AROUND PONTARDAWE

THE THIRD SELECTION

COMPILED BY

THE PONTARDAWE HISTORIANS

JEFF CHILDS *Jeff Childs*
EUGENA HOPKIN *Eugena Hopkin*
CLIVE REED
EURIG ROBERTS
KERI THOMAS *DK Thomas*
EUNICE WILLIAMS *Eunice Williams*

The History Press

An evocative image of the towering chimney stacks of Pontardawe steelworks, taken in the first half of the twentieth century. The stacks represented a monument to the town's industrial heritage and were demolished in 1965. Three steeplejacks are shown repairing the chimney; a hazardous job undertaken with little protection, in the days when health and safety standards were minimal.

First published 2013

The History Press
The Mill, Brimscombe Port
Stroud, Gloucestershire, GL5 2QG
www.thehistorypress.co.uk

© The Pontardawe Historians, 2013

The right of The Pontardawe Historians to be identified as the Authors of this work has been asserted in accordance with the Copyright, Designs and Patents Act 1988.

British Library Cataloguing in Publication Data.
A catalogue record for this book is available from the British Library.

ISBN 978 0 7524 8622 2

Typesetting and origination by The History Press
Printed in Great Britain

CONTENTS

ACKNOWLEDGEMENTS

We are very grateful to Gareth Edwards CBE for kindly agreeing to write the foreword and to all those named below.

Photographs and other images provided by:

Biteback Publishing Limited; Evelyn Bowden; David Bowen; Eurwen Bowen; Jeff Childs; Ena Dawson; David Davies; David and Mair Davies; Douglas Davies; Islwyn Davies; Nest Davies; Wynne Davies; Keith Day; Mrs Ray Edwards; Barry Flint; Lynne Gent; Huw George; Glamorgan-Gwent Archaeological Trust; David Griffiths; Eugena Hopkin; Doreen Howard; Islwyn James; Rhydwen James; Gareth Jeffries; Tudor Jeremiah; Elizabeth Jones; Parch. Gwyndaf Jones; Islwyn Jones; Meinir Jones; Phil Jones; Sandra Jones; Trevor Jones; Doris Joseph; Gwen Lewis; the late Catherine Lloyd; Sylvia Lloyd; Ian Milne; Heulwen Morgan; Jenny and John Morris; National Museum Wales; Ordnance Survey; Ken Plant; Marilyn Pugh; Edwina Ranft; Clive Reed; William E. Rees; Huw Roberts; Royal Commission on the Ancient and Historical Monuments of Wales; South Wales Record Society; Betty Thomas; D. Gwyn Thomas; Illtyd Thomas; Keri Thomas; Nigel Thomas; Welsh Government; Beti Williams; Bob Williams; Emlyn Williams; Eunice Williams; Huw Williams; Iris and Tal Williams; Janice Williams; Meinir Williams.

Other information and assistance from:

Jean Ayres; Edward Bevan; Islwyn Davies; Edwin Hartland; Dr Andrew Hignell; Dr Peter Jackson; Rhian Jones; Ryan James; Tom Jones; Delyth Lewis; Robert Lewis; Les Nixon; Raymond Owen; Siân Phillips CBE; Pontardawe RFC; Joseph Rengozzi; Ann Thomas; Marian Thomas; Steve Williams; Tom Williams.

This volume is dedicated to the memory of Gordon Williams; Pontardawe historian, colleague and friend.

Gordon Williams (1933–2008). Gordon was the first Chairman of the Swansea Valley History Society, later serving as President. He was also an accomplished photographer, gardener and horticulturalist, held in very high regard by all who knew him.

FOREWORD

I was very pleased to be invited to write this foreword to the new selection of images relating to Pontardawe and district. The area is part of my heritage and has very special and fond memories for me; both as a boy making the epic journeys by bus from Gwaun-Cae-Gurwen to Swansea and Neath, and then as a teenager attending Pontardawe Technical School. Even today, when I travel through Pontardawe en route to visiting my mother in GCG, I instinctively sense the aroma of fish and chips or hear the sounds of the sixties reverberating in my head.

Travelling through the district today, I am strongly mindful of how beautiful the valley is and how its industrial nature, which I well remember, is no more. From a very young age the whole area held a sense of adventure for me; none greater than when it came to fishing, with many a happy hour being spent on the River Tawe and its tributaries. The district was also a key centre for cycling and I have vivid memories of cycling from GCG through Cwmgors, past Abernant Colliery, then down to Pontardawe Cross and beyond. I also recall the return journey and the long, hard slog up Gelligron Hill! Other cycling trips took me to the Baran for whinberry-picking and the Barley close to Llangiwg Church and the golf club.

As a young miner's son, village life was all-encompassing and, in itself, insular. Having originally walked to school when living in GCG, suddenly there was great excitement at the prospect of travelling by bus to school in Pontardawe. It is well documented that Pontardawe Technical School and particularly its PE teacher, Bill Samuel, provided me with the building blocks for my later career. But equally invaluable were the new experiences the school opened up for me, such as meeting other pupils from such far-flung regions as Clydach, Gorseinon and Ystalyfera, which made me acutely aware that the universe was a little bigger than I had realised. As schoolboys, we used to organise sporting events ourselves, be they rugby or soccer, and it was always exciting to travel to new places such as Clydach, Trebanos and Godre'r Graig.

Closer to the school, and indelibly linked in my memory, were the 'hundred steps' which I ran up many times as part of my PE and training routine. This was a tough but ultimately beneficial assignment and I can assure you that the number of steps was far closer to two hundred than the name suggests. Whilst the 'hundred steps' are still there, sadly the school is no more. There is no doubt, however, that it was heavily influential in my future journey in life, whether viewed in terms of teenage development, widening my horizons or gaining new friendships. It was an experience I shall always be grateful for and one I will never forget.

Gareth Edwards CBE, 2013

A Gareth Edwards XV versus a Cwmtawe Past and Present XV played on 11 April 1974 at the Cwmtawe School Rugby Ground, Pontardawe. Gareth Edwards closely monitors the situation as Kim Davies gets the ball moving for Cwmtawe. Elgan Rees (from Trebanos) is the player with his back to the camera, and Dai Morris is blind-side wing forward. Other international players in Gareth Edwards's XV included Gerald Davies, David Duckham and John Spencer.

Davies & Co., general merchants' store on the Cross, Pontardawe *c.* 1925. The business was known locally as 'Davies the Ironmongers'. Built in 1854, it was one of the first shops in Pontardawe supplying the growing community with building materials and household items such as baths, buckets, wash tubs, oil lamps and wallpaper, as well as vegetable and flower seeds. As general merchants, Davies & Co. provided supplies to industrial concerns including nuts and bolts, colliers' shovels, mandrels, small tools and tinworkers' aprons. All stock was transferred to the shop from canal barges.

INTRODUCTION

The following extract from *The Pontardawe and District Year Book and Diary* for 1912 gives an evocative description of Pontardawe in its heyday. It is taken from an essay sent in to the Mount Elim Eisteddfod, 7 October 1911:

Situated as it is between the source and the mouth of the river on which it stands and at a point where communication is direct between the Amman and Neath Valleys, Pontardawe, by virtue of its geographical position, is favourably situated for commerce. Hence, its position with relation to its environments becomes a strong factor in deciding its future welfare.

The town thus forms a centre or pivot, with which the surrounding districts are closely connected. It is conveniently situated for trade; for the transaction of public and private business; for the importation of neighbouring agricultural produce and industrial products, and for the distribution of such commodities; either wholesale or retail. Industrially, its position in the centre of mining valleys makes its access to the various collieries very easy, and provides it with sufficient coal and other motive power for the upkeep of various trades and industries.

Pontardawe is the centre of a hive of activity. In the most populous parts, including Ynysmeudwy, Rhos, Alltwen and Trebanos, the majority of the male population follow their employment as colliers or tinplate workers, whilst in the more remote districts of Rhyd-y-fro, Baran Mountain, Gellionen and Marchywel, agricultural work is carried on. However in most cases farms are not very large, and the employees are frequently members of the family living at the farm.

To meet the wants of its inhabitants who are engaged in the various trades and industries, and also to act as a kind of market for the produce of the outlying agricultural districts, the town of Pontardawe is naturally a great trading centre.

Such a state of affairs brings about an interchange of commodities, which is of vital importance to the community. In fact, almost every commodity necessary for daily life of the people and for the upkeep of the community is procurable. Thus instead of Pontardawe being dependant on Swansea, as in days of yore, it has now become greatly self-supporting, and is like Swansea, a centre with its outlying districts dependant on it.

This description of Pontardawe in its heyday in the early twentieth century indicates how the town had developed over 150 years. Today the heavy industry has gone and it is difficult to visualise the extent of the industrialisation that took place in this part of the Swansea Valley and particularly in Pontardawe.

We trust you will enjoy the compilation and the photographs and images included in this new volume.

The Swansea Valley History Society was founded in 1978 to record the rapidly changing face of the Swansea Valley, and particularly Pontardawe and district. An early committee of the SVHS is shown above. From left to right, back row: Graham Davies, Philip Jones, Glanville Daniel, T.J. Davies (President), L. Thomas. Middle Row: Steve Williams (Secretary), Vernon Bruin, Gordon Williams (Chairman), Richard Jones, William Jones. Front Row: Eunice Williams (Membership Secretary), Elizabeth Jones, Anne Fryer, Meinir Jones, Gwen James.

Fel Pwyllgor, rydym yn gobeithio'n fawr iawn y bydd y llyfr hwn yn cael derbyniad gwresog gan ddarllenwyr yr ardal sy'n ymddiddori mewn hanes lleol. Mae'r llyfr yn adlewyrchu ein hymgais i roi ar gof a chadw yr agweddau hynny sy'n gwneud ardal fel Pontardawe yn un hynod ac unigryw. Ein bwriad wrth gyhoeddi'r llyfr felly, yw eich ysbrydoli chi'r darllenwyr i fynd ati i'w ddarllen yn awchus ac i ymchwilio'r gorffennol sydd mewn llawer dull a modd wedi llunio'r presennol.

1

PREHISTORY

The earliest known prehistoric remains found in the Pontardawe district originate in Neolithic times and date from around 4,000–2,500 BC. They relate to chambered tombs, of which there are two notable examples in the area: at Pen-yr-Alltwen and on Mynydd Carnllechart. The former, lying just below the former Pen-yr-Alltwen farmstead, is notable for its scale of construction, as is the one on Mynydd Carnllechart, which although in a collapsed state, remains impressive. Lying close to the Neolithic tomb on the latter mountain is a ring cairn comprising stone slabs, at the centre of which was a rectangular central cist dating from the Bronze Age (2500 BC to 800 BC). This is the famous Carn Llechart stone circle, known locally as 'Cerrig Pikes'. Dating to the second millennium BC, it comprises twenty-five outward-leaning stone slabs and has a diameter of approximately 14m. The cist or grave has long been disturbed, whilst its capstone, which would have been covered by a mound of stones and earth, has disappeared. The monument is referenced in one of Britain's earliest antiquarian books, William Camden's *Britannia* (1695 edition). Mynydd Carnllechart is indeed littered with cairn remnants notably on Brynchwith Farm. There are also a number of cairns on Cefn Gwrhyd, including Carn Llwyd, which at one time is said to have rivalled Carn Llechart in terms of size and scale.

The Bronze Age saw the development of more advanced bronze implements, with weapons becoming increasingly common. An axe head, now in Swansea Museum, was allegedly part of a hoard found on Mynydd Marchywel and is an excellent example of its type. A bronze 'leaf bladed' sword was also found with the axe and is regarded as one of the best examples found in Wales. Moreover, various Bronze Age standing stones are present in the district with those on Cefn Celfi Farm, Rhos, being formerly amongst the most prominent. Today, only small portions of the stones remain due to damage by farmers and past revellers. The thirteenth-century *Black Book of Carmarthen* makes the following reference to the stones: *Etri bet yg kewin kelvi* (*y tri bedd yng nghefen celfi*, the three graves in Cefen Celfi). The book names the heroes of the graves as Cynon, Cynfael and Cynfeli. Standing stones can also be found on Cefn Gwrhyd, including one near to Gwrhyd Chapel, the latter slab having been set into a dry stone wall on the edge of a field.

In the Iron Age (800 BC to AD 43) Celtic metal work became established as an insular form of expression and the later Iron Age metalworkers developed styles to decorate swords, scabbards, shields and horse harnesses. A segment of horse harness with red enamel pressed into the metalwork was found in Lon y Wern, Alltwen, and probably dates to between 50 BC and AD 50. It is now housed in the National Museum Wales, Cardiff.

Evidence of Dark Age culture can also be found in the district. The Gellionen Stone was probably the shaft of a disc-headed cross or wheel cross. It was carved from the local Pennant Sandstone in about 900 AD and stood on Mynydd Gellionen. The piece of the stone that survives shows what is apparently a Celtic priest with his hands raised in prayer and wearing a long cape with his hair cut short in the monastic style. The stone was subsequently used in Gellionen Chapel as a horse-mounting block and later, as a building block. When the chapel was rebuilt in 1801, the stone was set into an outside wall of the building. In 1965 the significance of the stone was recognised and it was removed to Swansea Museum. A replica carved in slate was set into the wall of the chapel on the site of the original stone.

In the porch entrance to Llangiwg Church, there is a fine example of a wheel cross head which is conservatively dated to the same century as the Gellionen Stone. There is speculation that this wheel cross head, together with the Gellionen Stone, may have formed the single wheel cross reported by the famous seventeenth-century antiquarian Edward Lhuyd as being located on Mynydd Gellionen. It is possible that this cross could have belonged to Llan Eithrim, a pre-Reformation daughter church of Llangyfelach, located on the slope of Mynydd Gellionen near Clydach.

This brief account represents but a small part of the rich cultural prehistoric heritage located on the upland areas surrounding Pontardawe.

Neolithic chambered tomb, Mynydd Carnllechart. The site is loosely dated to the late Neolithic to early Bronze Age. The stones have been displaced but experts believe that this is a tomb structure. The tomb is located some 100 yards north-west of the more well-known Carn Llechart stone circle. (Royal Commission on the Ancient and Historical Monuments of Wales)

Neolithic chambered tomb, Pen-yr-Alltwen. The tomb comprises two chambers; both constructed from large upright sandstone slabs. It was originally covered by a large capstone, now shifted to one side.

Cefn Gwrhyd standing stone. The rectangular sandstone monolith is now recumbent. Lying equidistant between Gwrhyd Uchaf and Pant farms, the stone is 1.4m wide by 0.5m thick, and when upright, must have been at least 4m high. A large stone projecting from the south-west side of the bank may be associated with the monolith. (Glamorgan-Gwent Archaeological Trust)

Carn Llechart stone circle. There are twenty-five slabs in the circle, up to 2.5m in length, with most leaning slightly outward. In the middle of the circle is a stone cist with its east side and capstone missing. One of the most impressive monuments of its type in Wales, it is said to date from the first half of the second millennium BC.

One of the three Cefn Celfi stones, part of a prehistoric burial area, located in the fields 300m west of Cefn Celfi Farm in Rhos. The stones have been severely damaged in the past. The *Black Book of Carmarthen*, written in the thirteenth century, refers to the three stones as representing the graves of three heroes, namely Cynon, Cynfael, and Cynfeli.

Segment of a horse harness found in Lon y Wern, Alltwen. The item comprises a lobed plate of metal elaborately decorated with red enamel inlay in the late La Tène (Celtic) art style. It is an unusually large example of a strap-union and was used to adorn a horse or chariot harness. (National Museum Wales)

A facsimile of the Gellionen Stone, incorporated into an outside wall of Gellionen Chapel, when the latter was rebuilt in 1801. The original stone, dating to AD 900, was probably the shaft of a disc-headed cross or wheel cross, carved from Pennant Sandstone. It was found in three pieces in a small cairn on Gellionen Mountain. It is said to depict a Celtic priest with his hands raised in prayer. In 1965, the stone was removed from the chapel and taken to Swansea Museum in view of its historic importance. The original is 2.5ft high and 1.5ft wide.

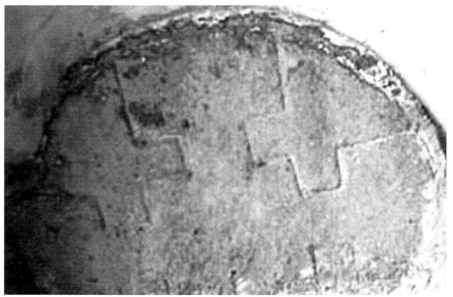

The wheel cross head stone located within the porch of Llangiwg church. It is conservatively dated to the same century as the Gellionen Stone. There is speculation that the cross and stone may have formed a single cross as reported by the famous Welsh antiquarian, Edward Lluyd. The cross may be linked to the medieval church of Llan Eithrim which stood near Gellionen Isaf Farm, Clydach.

2

MAPS AND GENERAL SCENES

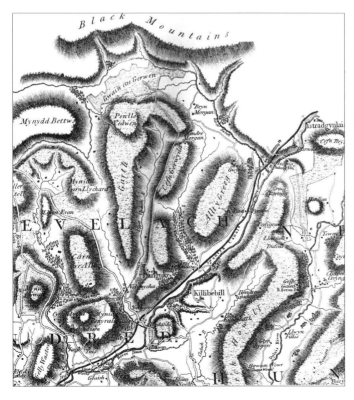

An extract from George Yates's map of Glamorgan of 1799 showing the district in pre-industrial times. Featured on the map are: 'Languke' and 'Killibebill' churches; Pontardawe; Alltwen; 'Place Killibebill'; 'Hendre Gradog'; 'Ynis Meudow'; Gellygron; 'Velynycha'; 'Mynidd Carn Llychard'; Garth; 'Penlle Vedwen' and 'Cefn Gerwydd' (Cefn Gwrhyd). The Upper and Lower Clydach rivers are also delineated, as are the River Tawe and the River 'Cledach', the latter in Cilybebyll parish. (South Wales Record Society)

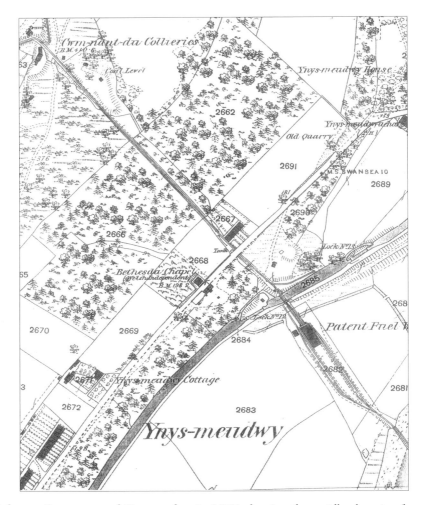

Ordnance Survey map of Ynysmeudwy in 1877, showing the rapidly changing face of an area once dominated by agriculture. The Swansea Canal, completed to this point by 1796, was still an important transport link for heavy industries in the valley, transporting coal, stone, brick, timber, iron and other materials. The two locks on the canal are numbers 12 and 13 in the canal company's order of sequence up the Swansea Valley. The patent fuel works was a new industry, only completed in 1875 by Warwick & Co. for the manufacture of 'patent fuel': a waterproof block of compressed poor-quality coal and pitch that gave out high heat. The coal was mined at the Cwm-nant-du collieries, whose tramroad conveyed the coal to the works and carried stone from nearby quarries to a wharf on the canal. Bethesda Chapel, Welsh Independent, was built in 1862 to serve the religious needs of the growing community. On the left of the map are two blocks of cottages, built in 1853 by the Ynysmeudwy pottery for their workforce. The nearby Ynysmeudwy Cottage was built in 1856. Alongside the tramroad are four cottages, again built in 1856; one of them was a named dwelling, Dan-y-Coed House. On the right of the map is Ynysmeudwy Uchaf Farm with its cow byre fronting the road. Opposite the farm is Ynysmeudwy House, built in 1848 by the Williams brothers, owners of the Ynysmeudwy Pottery. (Ordnance Survey)

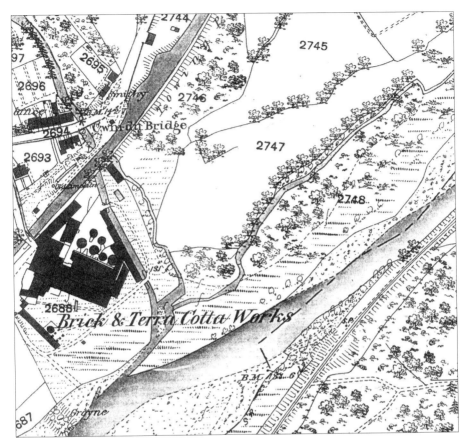

Ordnance Survey map of Ynysmeudwy in 1877. Dominating the page is the Ynysmeudwy Brick and Terracotta Works, originally Ynysmeudwy Pottery. Terracotta was the name given to decorative building articles, which were produced from the locally mined clay. The finest examples consisting of window pillars, lintels, sills and spacing columns, can be seen on the old Anglican schoolroom opposite the Ivy Bush Hotel in Pontardawe. Each week 20,000 house bricks and silica bricks were produced at the works during the 1870s. The works was put on sale in 1877 due to financial problems; no buyer was forthcoming and so it was closed. In 1879, Esiah Rees established a tinplate works at Ynysmeudwy, using the larger pottery buildings for that purpose. It later became the Bryn tinplate works. The buildings either side of the main road near Cwm-du Bridge were erected for the pottery workers in 1848. Thomas Vaughan, at one time the pottery foreman, became postmaster at the post office in one of the cottages. (Ordnance Survey)

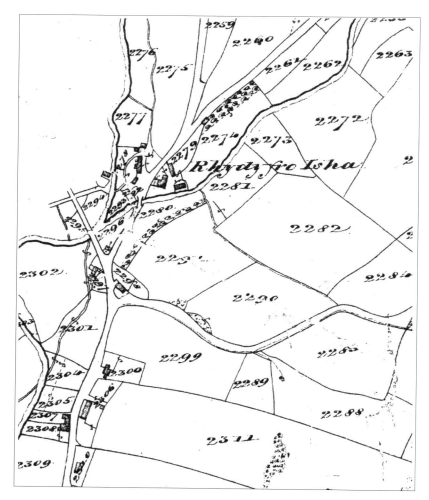

Part of the Llangiwg parish tithe map of 1840 for the Rhyd-y-fro area. The road running from the bottom of the plan is Commercial Road, leading to the Travellers Well public house at plot 2298. The split in the road shows the road to the Baran Mountain on the left, while the other road leads across the old bridge onto the former turnpike road. The original Saron Chapel can be seen at plot 2274, and what might be the old mill on plot 2292. The Royal Oak public house is on plot 2300, and the former (although not the first) post office is at plot 2307.

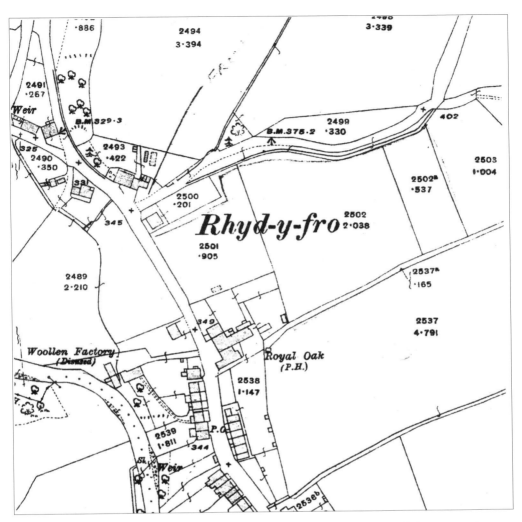

A 1918 Ordnance Survey map showing how the village has expanded over nearly eighty years. Much of the layout of the village that we see today has already been established on a linear pattern along Commercial Road. An additional mill has been established opposite the Royal Oak public house. More recent developments in the village include a new primary school and the Waun Penlan housing development. (Ordnance Survey)

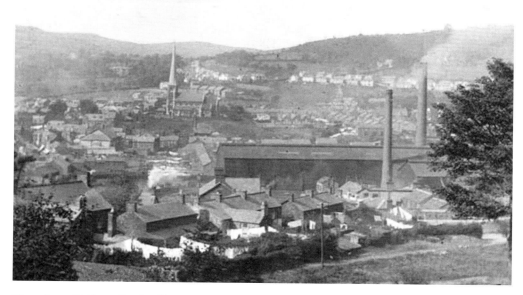

View from Dyffryn Road, Alltwen, *c.* 1950. The scene is dominated by the sheetworks which operated between 1921 and 1958, the site originally being developed in 1918 for the manufacture of alloy-steel round bars. The houses in the foreground lie on Alltwen Hill with Graig Llangiwg in the background (right).

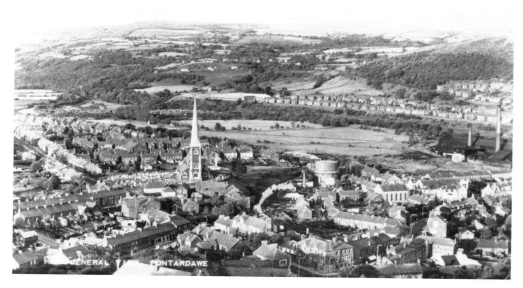

View from Graig Glynmeirch, *c.* 1960. The Cross Hotel (bottom), St Peter's Church and the gasworks are prominent. Part of the sheetworks lies centre right, abutting the undeveloped and generally boggy land that was formerly part of Ynysygelynen Farm. Railway Terrace, Alltwen, is in the background leading to the Imber factory.

Taken in 1952 from Graig-yr-Abbey, Alltwen (a reference to Neath Abbey, which farmed the mountain in earlier times) with Cilhendre Fawr farmhouse in the centre and Pen-yr-Alltwen to the right. The distinctive U-shaped nature of the glaciated Swansea Valley is clearly discernible. Mynydd Alltygrug is to the top right and the rim of the Carmarthenshire Fans is visible on the horizon.

A 1950s view of Graig Road and Dyffryn Road, Alltwen, taken from the start of Railway Terrace against the backdrop of Graig Alltwen. The large building, centre left, is the former Alltwen Infants School which now houses a community centre and is the base for Cilybebyll Community Council.

Ynysmeudwy, canal basin *c*. 1880. The area around the canal basin was a busy industrial setting at the turn of the nineteenth century, with stone blocks, paving slabs, coal, patent fuel, tinplate and lime all being produced. The tramroad bridge crossing the canal connected the Cwm-nant-Llici and Cwm-nant-du collieries with the patent fuel works. A short tramroad extension, from Cwm-nant-Llici quarry where paving slabs were manufactured led down to a wharf in the canal. The stone quarried at Ynysmeudwy was of excellent quality, and was used in the construction of the Landore railway viaduct in 1879 and Swansea East Dock between 1880 and 1882. The bridge was known as Bryn Bridge, after the tinplate works of that name alongside. The heavy industries of pottery and tinplate were situated to the right of the bridge. Alongside the upper lock is a waterwheel powered by the canal, and which turned a chaff-cutter. The locks were a very busy place in the past, with up to twenty barges waiting at the lower lock to journey up the canal. The last time a barge passed through the locks was in 1943. Original design by Clive Reed.

An RAF image of 1941 depicting part of Pontardawe and Alltwen showing much heavy industry: the sheetworks (bottom left), the steelworks (centre right) and the former chemical works (centre). The image is important for revealing a third crossing over the River Tawe which lay between the stone bridge and the 'wooden bridge'. This middle bridge (demolished by 1952) lay close to the boundary of the chemical works and originally connected with the Primrose Colliery tramroad which ran from Rhos. The picture also shows the rural nature of much of Alltwen. (Welsh Government)

The village of Rhos viewed from Pen-yr-Alltwen *c.* 1935 with the Rhos Infants School (opened 1908) prominent and Mynydd Marchywel in the background. The fields in the immediate foreground comprise parts of Pen-yr-Alltwen Farm. The houses shown lie on Plas Road (to the left of the school) and Neath Road (to its right). The farmland to the right of the school later became the Delffordd housing estate.

An oblique aerial view of Trebanos in 1971, with Swansea Road prominent and the Swansea Canal running parallel to it on the right of the photograph. The new housing development in Heol y Llwynau is under construction (left) above which runs the former railway, linking Trebanos with Felin Fran in Birchgrove via Clydach. This line was part of the Great Western Railway's attempt to connect with Brynamman, but only reached the Daren Colliery. This was the last line built by the GWR in South Wales.

St Peter's Church is particularly conspicuous in this shot of *c.* 1910, which includes: the South Wales Brewery; the Infants School; Horeb Chapel; Maes Iago; Church Street; Holly Street; the Public Hall and Institute; and a number of small-scale establishments on the gasworks' site. Some of Pontardawe's grand houses also appear, such as Brynheulog (centre right) with Gelligron House just above – whilst Glynteg (centre) and the chimneys of Glanrhyd (centre left) also appear. Penlan Farm can be seen top centre.

The 'one hundred steps'. The steps are in Coedalltacham and connect the footpaths at the bottom of the wood with Fairway Drive and Pontardawe Golf Club. The photograph shows Miss Peggy James on the steps in 1938. Although known as the 'one hundred steps', there are 191 steps in total. The legendary Gareth Edwards used to run up and down the steps twelve times during his lunch break whilst at Pontardawe Technical School. In 1988 a Canadian World Cup rugby union player, Ian Hyde-Lay, attempted the same feat but failed, only making it three times!

A view of Pontardawe in the early 1960s, showing the domination of the steelworks. The houses to the left lie on High Street, with those centre right being on Church Street. The former ambulance premises are to be seen on High Street (lower centre). The waste area in the foreground later became the site of the Pontardawe swimming pool, opened in 1974.

Two of Pontardawe's most distinctive churches. The building of All Saints Church (foreground) was financed by Arthur Gilbertson as a memorial to his father, William, who was buried in St Peter's Church whose unmistakeable steeple rises in the valley below. All Saints opened in September 1886 and held its last service on 2 November 1997, the property subsequently becoming a private residence. St Peter's Church was built between 1858 and 1860 and was consecrated in 1862. A number of celebrations were held in 2012 to commemorate its 150th anniversary.

3

FARMS

Hathren Rees with a stook of barley on Gellionen Ganol Farm in *c.* 1937. Hathren was the son of William Rees of that farm (*see* p. 49) and was organist at Gosen Chapel, Trebanos. The stook would be formed by the farmer placing bundles of sheaves together, which would be bound by lengthy strands of barley. Four to six stooks would be arranged to form a conical mound (mwdwl). One stook would then be turned upside-down with its stalks bound and placed over the mound. This would act as a helm to prevent rainwater from damaging the mound. When the weather was favourable, the mound would be thrown to the ground and spread out, with the stalks facing the wind to dry.

Gellionen Ganol Farm in 1937 when occupied by the Rees family. It measured 74 acres in 1838 when it formed part of the Ynyspenllwch estate and was bounded by Gellionen Isaf, Gellionen Uchaf, Ty'n-y-coed Uchaf, Ty'n-y-coed Isaf, Gwrach-y-llwynau and Graig Trebanos. The image gives a splendid example of a longhouse which survives in a modernised form today.

Cutting the corn harvest on Gellionen Ganol Farm, Trebanos, 1937. The horse is pulling a reaper and binding machine that cut the corn and processed it into stooks by tying parcels of the corn together. The corn was then placed into a 'mow', where it was left to dry, before the farmer gathered the mows and transported them in gambos to the farm yard for processing by a steam-driven combine.

Lygos, c. 1950. The property, measuring 30 acres, formed part of the Ynysarwed estate in 1838. The house lies on steep ground beneath Banc Sion and overlooks the Lower Clydach river. The property, as shown, was then in the ownership of the Green family who sold it in 1957 to Tom Plant, a mechanical engineer and former Spitfire pilot. Since his death in 1996, it has been totally restored by subsequent owners. Most of the land today is farmed by Hafod Wennol and Twll-y-gwyddil Farms.

Penlannau Farm was 93 acres in 1838 when it was owned by Lewis Weston Dillwyn, then of Sketty Hall and formerly of Penllergare, who acquired it in 1822 from the Briton Ferry estate. It is bounded by Henrhyd and Hafod Wennol Farms, and was previously a stopping-off point for drovers. A 1967 Royal Commission on the Ancient and Historical Monuments of Wales report described Penlannau as having an exceptional semi-circular projecting stair turret which 'has so far only been met once before in Glamorgan', at nearby Alltyfanog.

Betting Isaf comprised 72 acres in 1838 when it formed part of the Ynyscedwyn estate. Derelict for over thirty years, the front of the house faces Mynydd Alltygrug. There are remains of several outhouses and a former sheep wash on the site. Graig y Betting overlooks the property, which also abuts Betting Uchaf, Gwrhyd Uchaf and Cefn Gwrhyd.

Modernised in recent years, Cwrt-y-barriwns previously displayed signs of considerable antiquity and is said to have been the site of a manorial court baron. In 1838 it was owned by Maria Williams and others of Dyffryn, Bryncoch, and was 100 acres in extent. It abuts Cwmnantstafell (long ruinous), Bogelegel and Perthigwynion Farms, the latter now farming all these former separate holdings.

Pant is now derelict, being last occupied in the 1960s. It was 50 acres in 1838 when owned by Benjamin Howell, in whose family it had been since at least 1772. The property is farmed today by the adjoining Crachllwyn (Fawr), from which it is accessed. Crachllwyn also farms the long-abandoned Pistyll Gwyn, a former conventicle meeting house. (Royal Commission on the Ancient and Historical Monuments of Wales)

Godre'r Garth was a holding of 52 acres in 1838 when it was known as Garth Isaf and owned by Jenkin Davies Berrington, a Swansea solicitor. It was bounded by Mynydd y Garth, Garth Eithin, Garth Uchaf (the latter leaving little visible trace today) and Rhyd-y-fro Isaf. The old house (above) still stands, but is in a dilapidated condition. The successor farmhouse nearby dates from 1946. (Royal Commission on the Ancient and Historical Monuments of Wales)

Cwm Nant Lleici is a 14-acre farm today, but was 112 acres in 1838 when it formed part of the Ynyscedwyn estate and was bounded by Crachllwyn Fawr, Crachllwyn Fach, Pistyll Gwyn, Tyn-y-coed, Gellyfowy Fawr and Cefn Gwrhyd. Cwm Nant Lleici Quarry, dating to the late nineteenth century, lies close by and has seen extensive extraction of sandstone and gritstone, particularly important for road surfacing. Much of Cwm Nant Lleici is today farmed by Penydarren Farm.

Cilmaengwyn Isaf was 165 acres in 1838 when it formed part of the Ynyscedwyn estate, being bounded by Cilmaengwyn Ganol, Pentwyn, Gellyfowy Fawr, Ynysmeudwy Uchaf and Cwmtawe Isaf. It was sold by the estate in 1931 along with others in the vicinity. The farm now incorporates part of Cilmaengwyn Uchaf and Pentwyn, and along with Cilmaengwyn Uchaf and the long ruinous Cilmaengwyn Ganol, gives its name to the built-up district of that name.

Tarenni Gleision comprised 96 acres in 1838, when owned by John Bevan, who also possessed the adjoining and long ruinous Tarenni-y-cydau. The farm also abutted Brynysgallog, Ynys Wilhernyn and Bryncarnau. Forty acres are directly farmed today, the landscape being generally steep and inhospitable. The farm dates from at least 1543 and lies close to the former Tarenni Colliery coal tip, now overgrown with conifers.

Hendrecaradog was 398 acres in 1838 when coupled with the adjoining Bryncaranau, both farms being owned by the Cilybebyll estate. Only 4 acres today, Hendrecaradog's land is now farmed by the adjoining Wigfa. One of the oldest farms in the area, 'Hendre Cradocke' is referred to in a Cilybebyll estate record of 1539 as being bounded by Nant y Kellveyn to the north, Croes Oweyn to the east, Nant y Brychyeid to the south and the River 'Cleydach' to the west, all being in the manor of Neath Ultra and Cilybebyll.

Pen-yr-Alltwen was a holding of 55 acres in 1838, when it was part of the Gwyn estate and bounded by Alltwen Uchaf, Alltwen Ganol and Graig Alltwen. Demolished in the 1960s, this is the only known photograph of this large property and is one which shows its owner Llewelyn Bevan Williams and his wife, Elizabeth. 'L.B.' was the 'squire of Alltwen', such was his power and standing. A local quarry owner and builders' merchant, he moved in the same social circles as the district's leading families.

Alltwen Isaf comprised 87 acres in 1838 when it formed part of Howel Gwyn's extensive estate. His father, William, had acquired it from the Briton Ferry estate in 1821. The date-stone over the front door says 1831, but the farm is much older than this. Bounded by Llechau and at one time by Cilhendre Fawr and Pontardawe Mill Lands, much of Alltwen Isaf's holdings was later taken up by industry such as the Ynysfechan Colliery, Gwyn's Drift Mine and the Economic Hot Water Supply Co. Ltd.

4

THE SWANSEA CANAL

William Walker was a bargeman on the Swansea Canal. He was born in 1843, and probably commenced working on the canal in 1855 when he was twelve years old. He was still working as a bargeman when he was over seventy. He lived at No. 7 Glynmeirch Road (it was renumbered in *c.* 1965), Trebanos, and died in 1929. William was employed carrying coal from Abercraf to Swansea, bringing pit-props back to the mine on the return journey. The image of a teapot that was owned by William is known as 'Bargeware Pottery', and was very popular with bargemen in Great Britain during the Victorian era.

Lock-keeper's dwelling alongside Trebanos lock *c.* 1970. It was built by the Swansea Canal Navigation Company in 1827 as a home for the assistant lock-keeper for Trebanos locks. It was erected because Trebanos at that time was a small hamlet consisting of a few cottages and farms, none of which were close enough to the canal to be suitable for housing a canal employee. The building has only one small room, so the lock-keeper probably lived here alone.

William Walker with his barge and horse on the Swansea Canal, probably near Pantyffynon, Ystalyfera, *c.* 1914. The barge is 65ft long, nearly 8ft wide and fully loaded with over 20 tons of pit-props. Upright timbers have been positioned along the sides of the barge to increase its carrying capacity. The barge has just left a lock and is heading down the canal toward Pontardawe. William owned his own barge and horse, and took his horse home to his stable on Richardson Street, Trebanos, after each day's work. This is the only known photograph of a bargeman and a working horse on the Swansea Canal ever recorded and published.

Ynysgelynen Bridge in *c.* 1960, crossing the Swansea Canal at Holly Street, Pontardawe. The bridge took its name from the nearby Ynysgylynen farmstead, which stood close to where the Pontardawe Arts Centre is at present. Ynysgelynen translates into English as holly meadow; evidence that holly trees grew in the area in the 1790s when the canal was built. It was one of the original masonry bridges built across the canal in 1796.

Ynysgelynen Bridge *c.* 1960 showing the pronounced arched roadway. Note the diamond-shape weight restriction signs at either end of the bridge. They were introduced in the 1890s, after the coming of motor vehicles. Buses regularly used this bridge between 1920 and the 1960s, and often scraped the top of the arch as they went over the bridge, damaging the underside of the vehicles. In 1927, Pontardawe Rural District Council purchased the bridge from the canal owners. In 1960, the council applied for the bridge to be removed because it was a hindrance to bus traffic and demolished it in 1965.

Parc Cae'r Pandy, Pontardawe, 27 April 1988. The park, alongside the Swansea Canal, was created as a recreational area for families and young children on what had previously been the gas works site. The project was a joint venture between Lliw Valley Borough Council, British Waterways Board and the Pontardawe Civic Society, with financial assistance from the Mond Nickel Co. The park used natural materials such as timber and ropes to create wooden climbing frames, swings, slides and other activity features with a soft bark floor covering. Timber posts were used to create planters to make the park more attractive.

The official opening of Parc Cae'r Pandy on 27 April 1988. The park was the idea of the Pontardawe Civic Society, who strove to make Pontardawe a more attractive place for people to live. The Society's committee is shown with Len Blakesley and a Lliw Valley Borough Council employee on the left. Next to them are Keith Lascelles of the Mond Nickel Co., Glenys Lewis, Eunice Williams and Gwyn Davies. The Pontardawe Civic Society also raised money to illuminate St Peter's Church in Pontardawe, and was very supportive of the plans to improve the Swansea Canal.

Waun Coed canal terminal basin at Ynysmeudwy *c.* 1830. The Ynyscedwyn Iron Co. built the canal and dock facility in 1828 to enable its canal barges to transport coal from its colliery at Waun Coed to the ironworks at Ystradgynlais. At the dock facility were loading docks with coal drops to fill the barges, and a dry dock with carpenters' workshops and a blacksmith's shop for the repair of damaged barges. A tramroad bridge spanned the river, to enable the coal to be brought to the dock from the coal mine. The terminal basin is a listed structure on private property. (Royal Commission on the Ancient and Historical Monuments of Wales)

The remains of the Waun Coed branch canal, October 1983. The canal ran across Ynysmeudwy Ganol meadows and was about a quarter of a mile long. It is known locally as 'Crane's Canal', after George Crane, the owner of the Ynyscedwyn ironworks. It connected the Waun Coed dock with the Swansea Canal above Ynysmeudwy Ganol Bridge. The canal went out of use in the 1890s after the closure of Ynyscedwyn ironworks and the use of the railway instead of the canal.

The Swansea Canal at Ynysmeudwy, showing lock no. 12 and the lock-keeper's 'residence'. The canal was completed to Ynysmeudwy in 1796. In 1826, with the increase in the number of barges using the canal, the company built a new home for a lock-keeper at this location. The residence is only 10ft long by 7ft wide inside, has one small window and no toilet. After it was no longer used as a lock-keeper's home, it became a storehouse for the use of maintenance men on the canal. This is one of the oldest buildings in Ynysmeudwy.

Canal workers' cottages on Old Road, Ynysmeudwy, built in 1859 and known as Cwmshon Cottages. In 1920, William Thomas Williams, a lengthsman on the canal, owned the cottage on the left. His job was to maintain the canal between Ynysmeudwy and Pontardawe. This cottage is much superior to the residence alongside the lock. It has three bedrooms, two rooms downstairs, a kitchen and several large windows. Andrew Rickson, a stonemason of Ynysmeudwy, has since renovated the cottages. The cottage is typical of the buildings erected in Ynysmeudwy between 1850 and 1890 for workmen and their families.

The Swansea Canal at Ynysmeudwy in 1984 (top) and 1994 (bottom), showing the restoration work carried out by the Swansea Canal Society in that period. The Society was formed in 1981 and received funding from the Prince of Wales Trust for several projects. This was one of the larger projects completed at that time. The 1984 image shows the canal very narrow and shallow, with the towpath waterlogged and impassable to pedestrians.

The 1994 image depicts the canal as quite wide and deep, with an all-weather towpath suitable for walking and cycling. The barriers were introduced to keep motorbikes and horses off the towpath that were damaging the surface. The vessel in the 1994 photograph was the trip boat built by the Society.

Canal trip boat in Pontardawe July 1995. The boat is passing below Ynysmeudwy Isaf Bridge. Her name is David 'papa' Thomas, named in honour of David Thomas, born at Ty Llwyd Farm, Wernddu, in 1794. Thomas made one of the most important inventions in the iron-making processes of that era at Ynyscedwyn, and later became a pioneer of the American iron industry. Swansea Canal Society volunteers operated the boat during the summer months between Pontardawe and Ynysmeudwy, which proved very popular. Unfortunately, local youths destroyed the boat by setting it on fire in 2007.

Swansea Canal Society volunteers at Ynysmeudwy locks, 1991. From left to right are Clive Reed, Mike Clarke, Grant Duncan, Cath Fisher and Noel Watkins using the improvised 'bridge' to cross the canal lock. The Society won eight national awards between 1984 and 2008 for improvements to the canal's environment, including awards from the Civic Society, Shell Better Britain, Dŵr Cymru and Keep Britain Tidy, to name but a few. The Society relaid 4½ miles of towpath from Clydach to Ynysmeudwy, repaired all the historic bridges crossing the canal, dredged the waterway from Pontardawe to Ynysmeudwy, opened a heritage centre at Clydach and operated a trip boat at Pontardawe.

5

TRANSPORT

A London Midland and Scottish Railway 0-6-0 tank engine (no. 1123) at Ynysgeinon Junction, at the turn of the twentieth century, during a period of heavy snow. The locomotive was designed by S.W. Johnson for the LMS Railway and was built in 1875, being one of a number specifically built to replace the older locomotives of the Swansea Vale Railway. These locomotives were used regularly on the Swansea Valley line. By 1858 the line was being extended to Pontardawe, with a passenger service introduced on 20 February 1860. The railway was extended to Ystalyfera by 1861 and to Brynamman in 1868 for passenger traffic. Prior to the Beeching cuts, the railway was already in decline with passenger services being axed in 1950. By 1964, most of the railway had closed. The painting by Martin Davies shows the locomotive on the down line from Coelbren Junction. The track to the left of the picture is the main line from Ynysgeinon to Ystalyfera and Brynamman.

A typical motor vehicle of the 1920s outside the Cross Hotel, Pontardawe. There were a number of firms in Pontardawe that hired-out vehicles, including Lewis Bros of Grove Road, and L.W. Francis of High Street. These firms also hired-out charabancs for trips by local organisations.

A fine body of men comprising the Pontardawe Police Division outside what appears to be the Old Victoria Inn, c. 1910. The policemen are sitting in a Franson motor charabanc. The Pontardawe Division had jurisdiction over the Pontardawe Rural District Council area.

Pontardawe Cross *c.* 1925, showing a bustling scene. The two buses are from the South Wales Transport Co., which began operating in May 1914 as a subsidiary of the British Electric Traction Co. This view of the Cross remains essentially the same today, although the shops with canopies on the left have been demolished and replaced with public open space.

Bus at Hafod Wennol Farm, Rhyd-y-fro. The bus was built by Samuel Jones ('Sam yr Hafod') in 1934 with the chassis, cab and engine supplied by Francis Motors in Pontardawe. The bus conveyed Sam's own children and those from neighbouring farms on the Baran and Gwrhyd mountains to Rhyd-y-fro School. The bus had a conductor, Ifan John Morgan, of Brynchwyth Farm. This embryonic business developed into the well-remembered Glantawe Coaches based at Ynysmeudwy, then owned by Islwyn Jones and family. It was eventually sold to Diamond Coaches of Morriston, but the latter ceased trading in early 2011.

Humphreys' Garage, Swansea Road, Pontardawe. This family-run business operated a fleet of hire cars, in addition to its usual business of car repairs and petrol sales. The fleet could be commissioned for weddings or funerals, either individually or in greater numbers. The cars shown in the photograph are primarily Humbers, with what might be two Austins on the right.

Vintage motorcars at the old vicarage in Pontardawe in 1992. The smaller car is an Austin Big 7, a four-seat saloon with a 900cc side-valve petrol engine. It was restored by a Pontardawe car enthusiast in the 1990s. The larger car is a 1927 Austin 20 five-seat saloon, with a 3.6 litre side-valve engine. The Austin 20 had a large interior, and was used as a taxi, driving 1 million miles in that role. A local car enthusiast purchased it in about 1980, named it *Arthur*, and then drove it for another quarter of a million miles. It has never been restored.

A quiet Swansea Road, Trebanos *c*. 1925, with a South Wales Transport bus outside the Pheasant Bush public house. The second building beyond the pub was to become the Trebanos branch of the Co-operative Retail Society. The white cottage opposite the Pheasant Bush was demolished and replaced with Hudson's garage and petrol filling station. The scene remains much the same today, although the public house now houses the headquarters of Trebanos RFC, and the Co-operative has now gone.

Pontardawe railway station in 1937, showing the up platform and the goods yard behind, together with the goods shed. Just visible in the distance is the footbridge over the railway, for use by passengers accessing the down platform. The former sheetworks is prominent in the centre of the photograph. The site is now covered by the Tesco filling station.

The saddle tank locomotive *Pontardawe* was delivered to Gilbertson's steelworks in 1932 It was constructed by Beyer Peacock and Co. of Gorton, Manchester. The locomotive is seen here in its original livery, just before it left the factory for Gilbertsons's works. The locomotive was scrapped at the end of 1963. The company used approximately fourteen locomotives at different times with names such as *Renown*, *Glynteg*, *Victory*, *Lucy*, *Dorothy*, *Finedon* and *James Watt*.

Finedon, one of a fleet of 0-4-0ST OC steam locomotives which served the steel and tinplate works, taken near the locomotive shed in 1957. Built in 1941 by Andrew Barclay Sons & Co. Ltd at its Caledonia Works, Kilmarnock, it was acquired in February 1946 from the Finedon ironstone quarry in Northamptonshire, which was operated by Richard Thomas and Baldwins Ltd. The locomotive was scrapped in 1963. Some well-known loco drivers in the works were Bill Danaher, George Danaher, Sid Davies and Bob Fowler.

William Rees of the Gellionen Dairy, part of Gellionen Ganol Farm, delivering milk at Trebanos on the farm's dairy cart, *c.* 1937. The cart has pneumatic tyres, a sign of modernisation; the mudguards at the top of the wheels also indicate that not all the roads in Trebanos had been tarmacked. The lettering on the signboard was written in gold, outlined in red, stating that the milk was fresh.

Fire engine owned by the Pontardawe Rural District Council, *c.* 1939. The council was responsible for the provision of a fire service within its area. The Fire Services Act of 1938 combined the functions of 185 fire brigades throughout England and Wales, and imposed a mandatory duty on local authorities to provide fire-fighting equipment. The original fire station for Pontardawe was located to the rear of the former council offices in Holly Street, where the library is today.

Milestone Cottage at No. 48 Neath Road, Rhos, takes its name from the turnpike milestone built into the boundary wall of the property. The stone carries the legend of IV (4) miles to Neath. It was erected by the turnpike trust in around 1800 on the road running from Pontardawe to Neath. Mrs Eunice Williams, co-author of this publication, lived here at one time. Turnpike trusts were private companies who built and maintained the roads in Britain in the eighteenth and nineteenth centuries.

Postcard of Ynysmeudwy, *c*. 1910, depicting a courting couple enjoying a romantic view of the countryside at Ynysmeudwy. The company producing the card also used the same image for Pontardawe and other places, only changing the name on the sign. Local footpaths were important routes in each locality, and they were the responsibility of the parish council. There was an enormous mileage of such footpaths, and their upkeep was costly.

6

STEEL AND TINPLATE

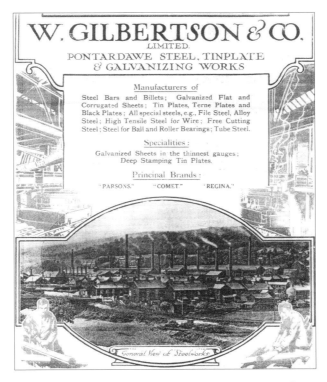

An advertisement for W. Gilbertson and Co. Ltd, Pontardawe, and its steel, tinplate and galvanising (sheet) works taken from the *Times Trade Supplement: The Industrial South Wales Section* edition dated Saturday, 29 October 1921. The advertisement lists all the major brands produced by the firm.

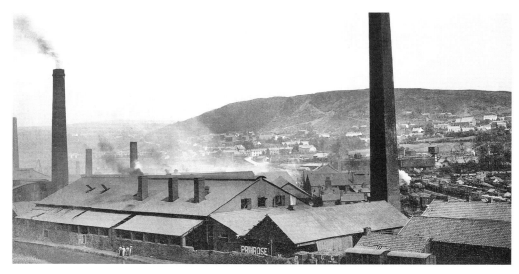

One of the earliest images depicting W. Gilbertson and Co., *c.* 1905. The original tinplate works dominates the foreground. One of the watchtowers of the chemical works can be seen in the background (right) whilst behind the right stack is the slag, manure and cement works and railway sidings. The coal wagon embossed with the *Primrose* name appears bottom centre near to those belonging to the Midland Railway and Gwaun-Cae-Gurwen Colliery Co. Bottom left is part of the Swansea Canal with female tinplate workers strolling along the towpath.

A 'Lowryesque' depiction of the steel and tinplate works at about the time of the First World War. The scene on the engraving has been exaggerated, there being less stacks in reality, or the Snowdonia range of mountains as backdrop. The administrative offices appear bottom right with the tinplate works to its left. Some of the buildings in the immediate foreground are the slag, cement and manure works. The billet and bar mills are shown (back, centre right), as are the casting pit and melting shop. The private branch railway line is shown (centre bottom) which connected the works with the LMS line at Pontardawe. (National Museum Wales)

Gilbertson's steel and tinplate works, Pontardawe, c. 1955, toward the end of its operational life. Steel was still produced, but on a much-reduced scale. The tinplate works (with white roof) continued production until 1957. There are chimney stacks of different heights and diameters, the tallest chimney in the foreground being 180ft high, which served the bar mill boiler house. In 1947, there were two stacks at 180ft high, one at 170ft, four at 140ft high, two at 120ft, three at 110ft and one at 80ft high. The last eight stacks were blown up in 1965.

Demolition of Pontardawe steelworks stacks on 1 August 1965. The operation was carried out by Birds (Swansea) Ltd of Morriston, purchasers of redundant works for demolition. There were eight remaining stacks on the steelworks site, which had stood forlorn following the closure of the works in 1962. Once demolished, the rubble remained undisturbed for a number of years until clearance of the site began in earnest in the early 1970s.

View of Pontardawe sheetworks (right) and steelworks, *c.* 1950, with Graig Glynmeirch and the Uplands in the background. The sheetworks' canteen is shown centre right, 'fronting' the houses of lower Herbert Street. The property on the far left (near side) is J.D. Owen's drapery, lying directly opposite the Pontardawe Inn or 'Gwachel'. The predominance of the steelworks is clearly illustrated, as is its close proximity to the town's residential and commercial properties.

Pontardawe sheetworks in the late 1950s, showing the extensive nature of the enterprise. The works was built in 1921 and closed in 1958, the stacks being blown up in 1961 and the site subsequently cleared. Fronting the works, with the white roof, is the canteen. Far left centre is the Pontardawe Inn or 'Gwachel', facing the drapery business of J. D. Owen on lower Herbert Street. The latter premises became the Continental Cafe in 1961. The advertising hoardings, which overlook the site of the former blacksmith's shop, hide the branch railway crossing gates at this point. The bridge over the River Tawe survives, but no longer takes motorised traffic.

The electric shop serviced the whole electrical requirements of the steel works, and also served as a maintenance department. The electric shop employed three shift electricians, three electricians' mates, one day-electrician, one day-electrician's mate working to a foreman with the latter working to the steelworks' engineer. Following the closure of the steelworks in 1962, the building was later occupied by Thomas & North, a heavy engineering firm. When it closed in 1985, the building remained empty, becoming derelict over time. It was destroyed by fire and finally demolished in 1996. The site now forms part of Lidl's car park.

The interior of the power house, Pontardawe steel works, *c*. 1950. The power house supplied electricity to the steel works, tinplate works, sheetworks and the Glanrhyd tinplate works via two 750Kw generators. It was located between the Pontardawe steelworks and tinplate works. The machinery in the power house was manufactured by the British Thomson-Houston Co.

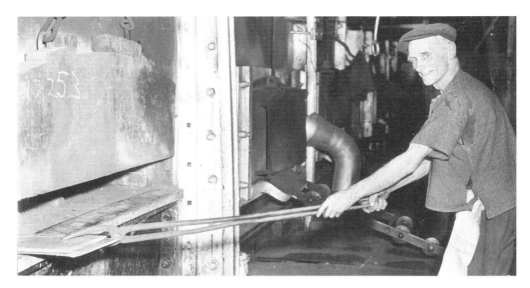

One of the hot mill team working at a furnace in Pontardawe tinplate works, *c.* 1950. This shows a man known as a 'second helper', who was one of the hot mill team. He is shown here wearing a *crys bach*, (a small shirt), the traditional clothing of those who worked in the hot mills. He is removing a pair of steel bars from the furnace, which was coal fired. The bars were referred to as 'tinbars', because they were used to make tinplate. The helper had to use very long tongs (6ft long) to remove the bars from the very hot furnace. The bars were then passed to the rollerman, who rolled them in the hot mill rolls.

Pontardawe tinplate works' hot mills, *c.* 1937. The works appear to be idle as a result of insufficient orders. This happened quite often in the Pontardawe works, as it did in other pack mills. There are no tools laid out among the machinery such as the tongs for the furnace man, the rollerman or the doubler. In the centre is a pile of about 150 'tinbars', stacked ready for the furnaces on the left. They were sufficient to make 1,200 sheets of steel for the tinplate process. On the right are the hot mill rolls.

This painting of 1955 by David Humphreys shows a rolling mill in the Pontardawe sheetworks. The large fly wheel provided the driving power for the machinery which contained rollers, with a large screw mechanism on top of the mill to adjust the space between the rollers. The men either side of the mill machine are feeding sheets of metal through the mill to achieve the correct thickness. David Humphreys lived in the former Ynysderw toll house.

Maintenance work at the Bryn tinplate works, c. 1934. The photograph shows the works craftsman/blacksmith, probably Bill Lockyer, repairing the worn end of a roll in the hot mill. He is using oxyacetylene welding equipment to melt the brass rod he is holding in his left hand to build up the worn end of the roll. The gas cylinders of oxygen and acetylene are lying on the bogey near the blacksmith. Maintenance work was carried out at the Bryn works on Sundays when the hot mill was not working. The chains visible are from the gantry crane that is holding the roll.

Presentation of a lamp stand to Tom Bevan, senior electrician in the electric shop on the occasion of his retirement in *c.* 1960. The presentation was made by Lionel Cooke (chief electrician). Also included in the picture are (from left to right): Gilbert Davies; William John Evans; John J. Thomas; Lewis Lewis; Tudor Beckett; - ? -; Bryn James; Alan Rees; and Huw Ebenezer (steelworks engineer). Tom Bevan, who lived in Rhos, was also a highly skilled model maker who won a number of prestigious competitions.

Presentation to Evan Davies of No. 16 Commercial Road, Rhyd-y-fro, on the occasion of his retirement from the sheetworks in the 1950s. The testimonial reads: 'I have great pleasure in handing to you on your retirement this document which records that you have given reliable and loyal service to the Company for 53 years. I wish you many years of happiness'. The presentation was made by Major David Randell (assistant manager of the Landore Group of works). Cliff Madge (general foreman in the sheetworks) is on the left, with Dan Young (TGWU representative) on the right.

Eight Pontardawe steel and sheet works veterans display their long-service certificates received in November 1956. From left to right, standing: I.B. Chilcott; A. Evans; G. Evans; Mrs H. Davies (Welfare Department); D. Maddock; D.D. John; D.W.H. Childs (Welfare Officer) and R. Woodley. Front row: C. Steadman; T.J. Canning (Steelworks Manager); G.E. Jones (Sheetworks Manager); and W.J. Evans.

Model of a horizontal steam engine used in the Pontardawe steelworks in around 1940 made from memory by Sam Howard of Godre'r Graig, who saw the engine in motion whilst employed in the steelworks. The engine is a two-cylinder machine used to drive the mills in the bar mill department. The bar mill rolled ingots produced in the works, into long, square-section bars. This is a rare example of such a machine and because of its provenance (being produced by a former employee), it was accepted by the National Museum Wales into its national collection.

Pontardawe steelworks 'C' furnace *c.* 1910, the smallest of the nine furnaces in the works was charged (or filled) by hand. Scrap metal came from other suppliers in the country, and because the scrap often contained impurities that were detrimental to the finished steel, specialist metals were added to the furnace to counteract such effects. The man second from the right appears to be holding a bar of special metal for that purpose. The furnace team are, from the left: Mr Brooks (Thomas Street); Bert Jenkins; Davy Bowen; Mr Salter; Mr Brooks (the leading hand); Frank Williams; and Mr Jenkins (Church Street).

Millwrights in Pontardawe steelworks, *c.* 1920. Millwrights installed and repaired machinery and equipment in the mills of the steelworks and tinplate works. To the right are end sections of rolls, which give an indication of their size. These rolls were approximately 18in in diameter. The millwrights would replace rolls when they broke. If the bottom roll fractured, the men would have to support the top roll with large jacks. The steam crane was used to lift rolls into position.

7

OTHER INDUSTRIES

A conspicuous feature of the Pontardawe chemical works was this wooden watch tower erected in *c.* 1910 by W. Jenkins. The works was founded in 1851 by Jacob Lewis and survived until 1931. It was independent of the various steel and tinplate concerns in the Swansea Valley, but was a key supplier of sulphuric acid to the tinplate industry for use in the pickling process. The last vestiges of the Pontardawe chemical works were cleared in around 2000, and the site today is largely covered by a Tesco store, which opened in 2005.

Part of the Pontardawe chemical works showing various buildings and the watch towers in
c. 1936 – five years after the works closed. The building in the foreground lies parallel to
the former Primrose tramroad, at the point where the latter crossed the River Tawe, over the
bridge just discernible on the left and which was demolished before 1952. The immediate
right, where the embankment is shown, was the site of the former Ynysfechan Colliery. This
is now part of the Tesco site.

A busy scene at the southern end of the former Pontardawe railway station in 1909, with
the Gilbertson's steel and tinplate works in the background. The wooden structure supports a
piping system, conveying a solution of vitriol from the chemical works to the tinplate works
for use in the pickling process. The lettering on the trucks shows that various owners of works
transported their goods on the Midland railway. There is a Midland Railway truck, a Primrose
Colliery truck and a Lewis G. Lewis truck, the latter belonging to the chemical works.

Pontardawe woollen mill, located at Maes Iago on the eastern bank of the Upper Clydach river. In 1838 Evan Davies was the master weaver who, in 1851, employed five men there. The machinery was worked by a large water wheel but was disused by 1901. In 1871, the mill was managed by David Thomas, and in 1891 the operator was Thomas Humphreys. The Humphreys family also had a candle works, which formed part of this structure.

Gelligron mill *c.* 1950, which being over 350 years old, was starting to deteriorate due to lack of use and maintenance. Local mills such as this were superseded by larger more efficient concerns, capable of producing hundreds of tons of flour per day. The building is a shell today, although the mill stones are visible and some of the stone walling that retained the mill pond can be seen, as can the wheel pit.

New Primrose Colliery, Rhos. A tramway ran from Rhos through Alltwen (Lon y Wern) and across the River Tawe, close to the chemical works, joining up with a private canal owned by the Primrose Colliery Co. which connected to the Swansea Canal. Much of the tramway route can still be walked today. The colliery was part of the Primrose concern, owned by John Morgan and Griffith Lewis. In 1869 the South Wales Primrose Coal Co. Ltd was established, which owned the New Primrose Colliery in Rhos as well as several others in the vicinity. The New Primrose opened in 1895 but had closed by 1908. The nearby Old Primrose was (finally) disused by 1942.

The first tram of coal from the Graigola seam of the New Glyndole Colliery, in 1923. The colliery was situated near Glyndolau Farm, Gellinudd. Included in the photograph are: Herbert Griffiths (left), who was the father of Tudor Griffiths (second left) and David Griffiths (right).

The official opening of the Pontardawe Industrial Estate on 24 February 1967 at the entrance to the Alloy. Pictured left to right: Ivor Davies, MP., Parliamentary Under Secretary of State, Welsh Office; Rt. Hon. Douglas Jay, MP., President of the Board of Trade, who unveiled the plaque to commemorate the occasion; Cllr Gilbert Lake, Chairman of Pontardawe RDC's Industrial Development Committee; Cllr John Davies; Islwyn Hopkin (news reporter); Cllr Percy Davies, Chairman of Pontardawe RDC; D. Glyn Meredith, Clerk to Pontardawe RDC and Cllr Elvet H. Williams, Vice Chairman of Pontardawe RDC.

The opening of Pontardawe Rural District Council's Industrial Estate South Section on 17 September 1971 by the Secretary of State for Wales, the Rt Hon Peter Thomas QC, MP. The ceremony took place directly opposite the former steelworks' administrative offices (later Ty Mawr). Mr Thomas is seen here (right) with Dan Young, unveiling a plaque in recognition of the work undertaken by the Pontardawe Rural District Council following the reclamation of the former steelworks site. The plaque has now been removed (whereabouts unknown), following the demolition of the former tinplate works in 2011.

A road-widening gang, working on road improvements at Rhyd-y-fro in 1931, just below the Travellers Well public house. Glamorgan County Council undertook improvement works to this stretch of road, including the old Rhyd-y-fro bridge (*see* below) in order to widen and straighten the narrow bridge. The motor van in the bottom photograph is crossing what was the old bridge, and practically fills up what was the old carriageway.

In 1950 the Pontardawe Rural District Council introduced the first Building Apprenticeship Scheme in the country when work commenced on the construction of houses in Brynawel, Pontardawe. The top photograph shows Sir George Gater, Chairman of the Scheme, on a visit to Pontardawe in that year with some of the apprentices and dignitaries from the council. The bottom image shows two of the last houses to be completed. The quality of these houses compared favourably with the social housing being built on the continent after the Second World War.

In 1921 the Great Western Railway was constructing a line from Felin Fran to Gwaun-Cae-Gurwen and the scene depicts part of the line under construction at Rhyd-y-fro. The railway shown is a temporary track, used to transport materials to the main construction works. Also significant are the prefabricated huts shown, being accommodation for the navvies working on the railway. They were located on the Baran road just north of the river bridge over the Upper Clydach river. Remarkably, one of these huts has remained as a private residence but may soon be demolished to make way for a modern dwelling.

David Davies & Sons, builders, *c.* 1950. The firm was founded in 1875 by Henry Davies, a carpenter, and was in existence for some 100 years, being based at the bottom of Park Road, on Lon y Wern Alltwen, with a small office adjacent to the Rock public house. It made its reputation through building council housing for both the Pontardawe and Ystradgynlais Rural District Councils in the 1920s. Between 1919 and 1971 it constructed 674 houses for Pontardawe RDC and some 270 houses for Ystradgynlais RDC, as well as many private dwellings.

A view of the goods yard at Pontardawe railway station, *c.* 1910. The gentleman with the white collar nearest the cart is William Richards who owned a business that made wooden clog bases. He would purchase an area of woodland, cut the timber and transport it on the cart to his works at the rear of station. Timber would be cut and shaped into clog bases and when a truck load was ready, these would be transported to the Midlands so that leather uppers could be attached.

Station staff, Pontardawe railway station 1947. The small cabin structure was used to contact the north signal box, which was located beyond the goods shed and the road overbridge. Back row, left to right: George Underhill (foreman of the marshalling yard); Tom Wheel (stationmaster); and Trevor Jones. Front Row: W.R. (Dick) Evans (junior clerk); Joyce Hopkin (clerk); and Gareth Jenkins (junior porter).

The 'Old Brewery' in Pontardawe, *c.* 1850, situated between the Swansea Canal and High Street, drawn by Mike Jones. This was the third brewery to be built in the village and was constructed by John Jones of Ynysderw Farm in 1837. It was erected alongside the canal to allow barges to deliver beer to the public houses along the canal side. This is one of the oldest buildings in Pontardawe.

Mr Burley (left) and Mrs Bentley of Messrs Berlei (UK) Ltd, Pontardawe, discussing administrative problems with H.D.M. Davies (left), Divisional Youth Employment Officer, and Mr Curry of the Youth Employment Bureau, Pontardawe, at the Berlei factory in Church Street in 1964. The factory was purpose-built following the demolition of the Pavilion cinema. Berlei ceased production in 1982, and the premises are currently partly occupied by a double glazing firm and a builders workshop.

Walter and Rachel Joseph (top photo) at the Egel Dairy, Rhyd-y-fro, *c*. 1950. Walter (1886–1956) was formerly a miner, and set up the dairy when he married Rachel just after the First World War. The dairy cottage, situated alongside the main road near the Traveller's Well public house, consisted of a kitchen, scullery, pantry and small parlour with two rooms upstairs. Their cows produced sufficient milk to enable them to have a milk round in Rhyd-y-fro, which Rachel delivered. Rachel also made ice cream that she sold in the afternoons from their horse and cart. The bottom image shows George Joseph, Walter and Rachel's son, at the dairy in c. 1935.

David Griffiths outside his warehouse located to the rear of No. 52 High Street, Pontardawe. David was a wholesale merchant delivering vegetables and other goods to local shops and other premises. To the rear of the warehouse was a small slaughterhouse. Both buildings remain standing today. Many will recall No. 52 High Street as Nan's Fish and Chip shop.

The blacksmith's shop at Rhyd-y-fro showing John Evan Jenkins, the farrier, at work, c. 1925. The shop was located on the Baran road. The local blacksmith was a prominent member of the community as he undertook manufacture and repairs whilst the farrier shoed horses for the local farmers and gentry. The building remains today and is now occupied by a quad bike dealer.

8

STREETS

Lower Herbert Street, Pontardawe, *c.* 1930. The group of people, centre right, are standing outside Dai Mathews' Billiards and Snooker Hall. The first motorised vehicle is parked outside the branch of Lloyds Bank with the cenotaph (unveiled in 1921) clearly visible in the background. The second vehicle, in the far distance, fronts Laurel Cottage. The business of W. Morris, sculptor and monumental mason, operated where the Jubilee Club and its grounds stand today. The working-class housing to the immediate left (numbering 77 downwards), dates from at least the 1870s. It was still inhabited up to the mid-1960s but was subsequently condemned and demolished by the early 1970s. This part of lower Herbert Street was periodically affected by serious flooding as a result of the Upper Clydach river bursting its banks. Householders and businesses fought a valiant but unsuccessful battle against overwhelming odds, as the rising water level was unrelenting and left much damage and despair in its wake. It was not until the late 1970s that an effective flood-prevention scheme was put in place. Lower Herbert Street continued as far as the Pontardawe Inn or the 'Gwachel', and had domestic properties as well as commercial premises on both sides of the road. Among the latter were Arthur Evans's ironmongery; James the Baker's; the Continental Café (previously J.D. Owen's drapery and Midland House); Parry's newsagents; and a confectionary store run by Alice Powis and Edwin and Phyllis Harris. All of these buildings, as well as the domestic residences in this area, were demolished between the mid-to late 1970s as a result of the new road alignment that bypassed the town.

Taken *c.* 1905 when cyclists ruled the roost! The white wall to the left is the curtilage of Ynysygelynen House which was demolished *c.* 1907 to make way for the Public Hall and Institute. The shop to the immediate right was occupied between the 1950s and 1970s by Jack Farr and his butchery business. The road bridge over the LMS railway leading to Alltwen Hill can just be discerned centre left.

A view of Herbert Street *c.* 1910, close to the Cross, with the canal bridge in the foreground. The building on the right is the Temperance Hotel, under the proprietorship of D. Joseph, which is a hairdresser's today. Many readers will recall that from the 1950s the property was a busy grocery store owned by Donald and Myfanwy Jones.

An easily recognisable part of Rhos centred on Neath Road in *c.* 1930. On the left is the former Rhos Co-operative Society store lying opposite the turning to Plas Road, whose road signage survives today. The origins of the co-operative in Rhos date to the late nineteenth century and the building (a Premier grocery store today) remains the main commercial outlet in the village. The origins of Rhos as a community originate from the development of the Primrose collieries in the nineteenth century.

Commercial Road, Rhyd-y-fro, is the main thoroughfare through the village and originally linked with the former turnpike road from Rhyd-y-fro to Gwaun-Cae-Gurwen. The photograph, taken in the 1940s, shows the linear form of development along the road which characterised the early development of the village. The essential character of the road remains unchanged.

Not a car in sight! Davies the Ironmongers, the Cross Hotel and the Dillwyn Arms under the proprietorship of Elias E. Gape feature prominently, as does Griff. H. Davies's, a gentleman's outfitters in the premises later occupied by Parkhouse the newsagent's and subsequently Motorworld Ltd. The latter building was demolished in 2011 and the site cleared. Note the public urinal centre left.

Looking towards Swansea Road with Parkhouse the newsagent's in the centre and the hairdressing business of Jock McDade to the right, in the same complex. Davies the ironmongers stands to the right, opposite the small 'portico' entrance to the Cross Hotel and is the oldest building at the Cross.

High Street, Pontardawe, looking towards the Cross in the early 1950s. The drapery section of the co-operative store is immediately left while further down, towards the Cross and next to the vehicle, is the Home and Colonial store with the Cross Hotel next door. Beyond the Cross, on the right, is Parkhouse the newsagent's with Davies the ironmonger's lying opposite the hotel. The crowd of people on the right are waiting for a bus, this being one of the key pick-up points for such travel up the Swansea Valley.

Herbert Street from Pontardawe Cross c. 1920s. On the left is the Cross Hotel. Businesses on the same side as the Cross Hotel included a general store, a fruit shop, John Christopher Davies's drapery and outfitters and Phillips' butcher's shop. Opposite the Cross Hotel lay Trayler's newsagent's shop (later to become a post office), Phil Price's butcher's shop, Dr Watkin's surgery, the Grosvenor Café, a wool shop and Matt Harris' drapery shop. Also visible are the billboards on the side of William John Davies's ironmongery.

Derwen Road, Alltwen, *c.* 1910, close to its connection with Heol Penrhiwiau and Gwyn Street. Near the bottom of Derwen Road is the Pandy, a pre-1838 former mill which lies on the fast-flowing Llechau stream and which forms the parish boundary between Cilybebyll and Cadoxton Juxta Neath at this point.

Ynys y mond Road, Alltwen, 1952, looking towards Gwyn Street. The little boy on the left is Keri Thomas, who is awaiting the arrival of the milk delivery cart owned by Gwyn Lewis ('Gwyn the Milk') of Tyn-y-Cae Farm, Alltwen. Note the absence of traffic and compare it with today's thoroughfare, with its numerous speed bumps and parked cars.

Dedication ceremony for the fountain memorial to Howel Gwyn (d. 1888) at the Triangle, Alltwen, in 1895. The fountain was commissioned by local people and his tenants. The house in the background, Gwyn Villa, was at one time owned by the Howell family. It was demolished, *c.* 1970, to make way for a car park for Alltwen RFC.

The Triangle, Alltwen, 1908 with the memorial fountain to Howel Gwyn prominent. The latter was the owner of the largest estate in Alltwen. The Triangle became the site for the annual week-long agricultural fair that saw farmers buy and sell stock, as well as hire farm hands for the year. The last fair in Alltwen was held *c.* 1928. The site today remains much as seen here.

Swansea Road, Trebanos, *c.* 1930. A view looking toward Trebanos square. The view has remained relatively unchanged since the 1930s, except for the provision of a pavement on the right-hand side of the road. The houses are a mixture of small, late-nineteenth-century cottages and larger early-twentieth-century properties, all constructed of local stone.

Brecon Road, Ynysmeudwy, *c.* 1930, near to the junction of Brecon Road and Old Road. New Road was built to bypass Old Road sometime after 1850, hence its name. The houses on the right are typical of those built between 1900 and 1930. This is the original turnpike road of the early nineteenth century, the main Swansea Valley route to Brecon. Note the gas lamp near to where the women are standing. The corrugated sheet building beyond this is the 'Zinc School' for infants (it opened in 1909).

9

HOUSES AND BUILDINGS

This pre-1918 image shows the Capital & Counties Bank that preceded Lloyds Bank in Herbert Street. The Lloyds Bank that occupies the site today has expanded into an adjacent property, but the façade remains the same. The Capital & Counties Bank Co. was founded in 1834, and was involved in takeovers of other banks throughout the UK. It eventually had 473 branches. The bank also had foreign connections and participated in France, Canada, Mauritius and Brazil. The Capital & Counties Bank group was taken over by Lloyds Bank in 1918.

The Alltwen and Pontardawe Co-operative
Society store in High Street, Pontardawe, 1910.
The Co-operative drew its membership from
its customers, and its aim was to arrange bulk
purchases of goods at wholesale prices and pass
these benefits (the 'divi') on to its members.
The Society had branches in Alltwen, Pontardawe,
Rhos, Trebanos and Rhyd-y-fro. The Pontardawe
branch closed in the early 1980s.

The Home and Colonial in High Street, Pontardawe, *c*. 1910. Home and Colonial was
founded by tea-buyer Julius Drew and Liverpool shopkeeper John Musker. Tea was a key
product for the stores, which also sold dairy products, sugar, bacon and ham. There were
500 stores throughout the country at the turn of the century. A merger with Liptons and
others in 1924 brought together over 3,000 shops. The store in High Street closed in the
early 1970s and the site is now occupied by the Café On The Square.

Harris and Co., High Street, Pontardawe, 1902. This was a large furniture and general ironmonger's shop (known as the Emporium) owned by John Harris, with the furniture element located on the upper floors. Shortly after this photograph was taken, a devastating fire broke out and little was salvaged. The only fire brigade available was located in Swansea and it arrived too late. The building was eventually demolished and replaced with what became a Labour exchange (now flats for social housing).

Griff. H. Davies's, gentleman's outfitters, the Cross, *c.* 1910. The shop was subsequently occupied by Parkhouse the newsagents', and latterly by B & S Spares. The property, along with two other long-closed shops was demolished in 2011. The site is now public open space.

Waterfall Stores was located opposite the Victoria Inn on James Street. It was demolished in 1936 when James Street was widened. Standing in the doorway is Emlyn Davies, Annie J. Davies and Thomas Davies (the proprietor) next to him. The other gentleman is unknown. The family later moved the business to Church Street, still calling the shop Waterfall Stores. The premises was sited at the junction of Quarr Road and Church Street and is a private residence today.

Ceinwen Williams is seen here with her niece Margaret behind the counter of the 'Corn Stores', Pontardawe, in the 1950s. Although commonly referred to as the 'Corn Stores' it was officially known as the Pet, Poultry and Cattle Foods Store. The shop originally occupied the premises which later became the South Wales Electricity Board showroom, on the opposite side of James Street. It later moved across the road to new premises at the bottom of James Street and was well known as a general store which sold animal feed. In 1968 the business was taken over by Betty Williams, assisted by her husband Emlyn. The shop closed in 1983.

A view of what later became Harold Pierce's drapery shop (No. 6 Herbert Street), adjacent to the Cross Hotel in 1898. The window display is both interesting and intriguing; it shows what appear to be grapes and watermelons for sale. Note also the reflection of Adulum Baptist Chapel in the left-hand window. The shop is currently a hairdressers.

Jean Ayres in the doorway of *The West Wales Observer* offices, *c.* 1975. The *West Wales Observer* (and its successors the *Western Observer* and *Valley Star*) was produced between 1919 and 1978, having as its strapline 'the best paper for the Amman Valley, Swansea Valley and Dulais Valley'. Published every Friday, it covered a wide variety of news particularly in relation to Pontardawe and district. For many years the office was run by Miss Clara Chilcott, who also wrote the reports. The much-changed building still stands on Herbert Street, and today houses a boutique.

The Pontardawe Inn, *c.* 1920, Herbert Street. Despite its official name, the inn has gone by many names over the past century. In 1919, it was known as the Hotel Cecil, a meeting place of the Pontardawe Poets' Society. To most people in the area it is known as the 'Gwachel'. It is said that the word derives from the Welsh *gwrach* meaning 'witch', and refers to ladies of a certain virtue who entertained men with loose morals visiting the inn. Carved into the stonework of the adjacent Pontardawe bridge is a representation of a witch flying a broomstick.

'Gwachel' stone carving. The image is near the base of the old Pontardawe bridge, and was probably carved by one of the workmen from the blacksmith's shop located next to the bridge about a century ago. The carving has deteriorated because of weathering and is now barely discernable. The witch is flying a broomstick the wrong way round. The building depicted is the Pontardawe Inn, and appears as it was many years ago. The carving was discovered by Clive Reed.

A shop on Alltwen Hill *c.* 1910. This was one of several such premises on the hill and like so many others has been demolished and replaced with new housing and road improvements. Included in the photograph are James Watkin Jones, Flossie Jones and an unknown shop assistant in the doorway.

D.J. Phillips's newsagents' shop at No. 1 Graig Road, Alltwen, 1912, situated on the corner of Graig Road and Banwen Lane leading to Dyffryn Road. From left to right, are: David John Phillips (owner); Bessie Mathias; Phoebe Phillips (daughter); and Lizzie Phillips (wife). One of the notices in the window is announcing a meeting that will be addressed in Ystradgynlais by Kier Hardie, the first Independent Labour Party politician to be elected to Parliament in 1900. The shop has been demolished but the house adjacent still remains.

Butcher's shop, Neath Road, Rhos, *c.* 1930.
It was owned at that time by David John, whose
family came from Cefn Celfi Farm, Rhos. The shop
became a general store and haberdashery in
the 1940s and 1950s run by Elwyn Griffiths.
In recent times it sold bread and cakes but is
currently a hairdressers run by Gwen Hafod.

Des Davies ('Des the Butcher') with his wife Blyth and customer Lynne Charles at his
butcher's shop attached to Tyisha in Brecon Road. Des moved from Tairgwaith in 1931 to
live with his aunt and uncle in Brecon Road. Following his army service he carried on his
uncle's butchery business, which included overseeing the small slaughterhouse located in
a lane off Brecon Road. Des expanded the business to include a delivery service and the
provision of general produce. He also had a caravan storage area to the rear of the store.
The shop closed in the mid-1980s, and Des died in 2009.

Above: Celebrating the laying of two memorial stones for the construction of the new Saron Chapel, Rhyd-y-fro, in 1904. The chapel was built on land given by William Williams, MP of Maes y Gwernen Hall, Morriston and owner of the Upper Forest & Worcester Steel and Tinplate Works Ltd in that town. The total cost was £2,700. The stones were laid by Miss Violet Olwen Williams of Maes y Gwernen Hall, and Miss Mary Dulcibel Frances Gilbertson of Glynteg, daughter of Frank Gilbertson. The chapel was formally opened in August 1904 and remains a place of worship today.

Left: Proudly and imperiously towering over Pontardawe is St Peter's Church, known as the 'Cathedral of the Swansea Valley'. The year 2012 saw the church celebrate its 150th anniversary with a Holy Eucharist service held on 31 July. The spire was renovated in 2008 and is often illuminated at night time, being sponsored by individuals to mark special occasions in their lives. Donations for illumination also came from local organisations, with Pontardawe RFC being the first. The illumination was the initiative of the Pontardawe Civic Society. Some of the past and present members have included: Glenys Lewis; Bill and June Booth; Len Blakesley; Eunice Williams; Gwyn Davies; George Anderson; and John H. Morgan.

The Rectory, Cilybebyll, 1913. The Rectory, which served St John the Evangelist's Church, Cilybebyll, was a two-storey part-rendered building with slate gable roofs and a small, gabled slate porch. It is known as the Old Rectory today and comprises five bedrooms. Part of the property, which served as the rectory until *c*. 1983, is said to be over 400 years old, with electricity being first installed in the building in 1940. The successor rectory lies on Cwm Nant Llwyd Road, Gellinudd.

This house was known as Ochr yr Heol on Graig Road, Gellinudd and was located almost opposite the former Bryn Seion Chapel. The elderly gentleman sitting on the left is William Lewis, next to his wife Betty. The couple had fourteen children which included four pairs of twins. William worked in various collieries in the Gellinudd area and was employed in the Old Primrose Colliery in Rhos in October 1858 when fourteen men and seven horses were killed in an accident.

10

SCHOOLS

Headmaster and teaching staff, Rhyd-y-fro Primary School, 1925. The headmaster, D.J. Terry, is seated with Miss James, Miss Lloyd and Miss Williams standing. Since its founding in 1876, the school has had five head teachers and two acting heads. The original school closed in 1984 and a new purpose-built school was constructed at Waun Penlan.

Pontardawe Boys' School, 1956. Back row, left to right: Arwel Davies; Brian Day; Hywel Hopkin; Ieuan Pipe; Alun Davies; -?-; David Hughes; Jack Jones (teacher); -?-; -?-; -?-; Gareth Evans; Leslie Owen; Tommy Grove. Front row: Mansel Thomas; Richard Aldridge; Christopher Evans; David Jones; Daniel Griffiths; Lyn Brown; -?-; David Gwynfor Williams; John Lewis; Keith Carter; Gwilym Williams; Brian Holwill.

Pontardawe Girls' School, Standard 5, 1957. Back row, left to right: Joyce Eardley; Linda Sutton; Susan Bickle; Beryl Hodge; Judith Pearte; Christine Thumbwood; Mary Hartnell; Mary Margaret Williams; Helen Price. Third row: Barbara Gifford; Rosemary Strange; Eleri Pugh; Ann Strange; Nina Lewis; Nest James; Annette Scale; Cheryl Lewis; Priscilla Harries; Miss Wilcox (teacher). Second row: Gillian Williams; Margaret Jones; Ann Rees; Nita Griffiths; Ann McGarry; Christine Morgan; Mair Wyn Davies; Janet Hennessey; Eugena Williams; Lilian Martinson; Wendy Hill. Front row: Joan Lock; Iris Jones; Christine Rees; Iris Beddoe; Eryl Jones; Rhiannon Lewis; June Hapgood; Pat Thomas; Katherine Evans.

Ynysmeudwy Infants School (Zinc School), 1956. Back row left to right: Miss Margaret Thomas (teacher); David Jones; Brian Stead; Huw Lloyd; Keith Morris; Wynford Evans; Norman Davies; David Hodge; Cledwyn Hodge; David Thomas; Miss Morgan (teacher). Front row: Julia Davies; Janet Thomas; Annette Hewlett; Eirwen Parry; Marian Jones; Christine Martinson; Christine Daniels; Christine O'Halloran; Heather Thomas; Sandra Jones; Gaynor Evans; Beti Wyn Jones.

Pontardawe Infants School, 1960. Back row, left to right: Peter Eynon; Leslie James; Jeffrey Childs; Rhodri Jones; Allan Williams; Derek Beddoe; Miss Mary Jones (Headmistress). Middle row: Edward Bubb; Robert Lewis; Peter Jones; Timothy Thomas; Hugh Beckett. Front row: Gillian Davies; Paula Davies; Hilary Thomas; Mary Lewis; Barbara Jenkins; Kathleen Davies.

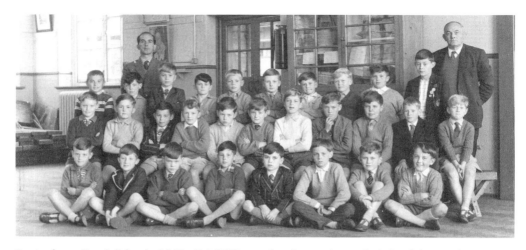

Pontardawe Boys' School, 1961. Tal Williams (headmaster) stands behind his students. Back row, left to right: Brian Epps; Eric Ginn; Stephen Rees; Royston Ginn; John Price; Garry Hapgood; David Hewlett; Barry Jones; Lionel Lewis; Ian Richards; Elwyn Ford (teacher). Middle row, left to right: David Evans; Wynford Evans; Ryan James; John Powell; David Reynolds; Stephen Morgan; Adrian Thomas; Brian Williams; Colin Rees; Stephen Evans; Allan Williams. Front row, left to right: Timothy Thomas; Paul Harries; John Lewis; Martin Davies; Rhodri Jones; Graham Bending; Huw Cotton; Huw Williams.

Pontardawe Secondary Modern School, 1964. Back row, left to right: Malcolm Whiteman; Robert Davies; David Reynolds; Julie Evans; Ian Davies; Wayne Isaac; Carol Russell; Huw Williams; Oswald Jones (headmaster). Second row: Mrs Betsan John (teacher); Laura Surian; Richard Jones; Gwenda Morse; Martin Davies; Rhian Lewis; Ryan James; Ann Howells; Keith Edmunds; Anita Hughes; Philip Jones. Front row: Stuart Lloyd; Carol Toner; Barry Jones; June Tipping; David Evans; Gloria Jones; David Lacey; Joy Williams; Terry Roberts; Barbara Rees; Hywel Griffiths; Malcolm Pritchard.

Pontardawe Grammar School *Cân Actol* group, winners of the under-16 competition at the National Urdd Eisteddfod held in Treorchi in 1947. Standing, left to right: Carrie Griffiths (accompanist); Iris Williams; Ann Powell; Siân Phillips; Margaret Daniels; Mair Rees; Dorothy Harding; Rita Morgan; Eileen Griffiths. Middle row, kneeling: Esther Davies; Marian James; Mair Williams. Seated: Sadie Thomas; Alice Thomas; Jean Jones; Nancy Evans; Ann Suff. The winners performed 'Y Ffair'. Siân Phillips was to become an internationally renowned stage and screen actress.

Pontardawe Grammar School's drama production of *Androcles and the Lion*, December 1950. Back row, left to right: Emyr Thomas; John Roberts; Alan Bailey; Vernon Lewis; Huw Jones; Jeff Lewis; Geoffrey Davies; Mervyn Williams; D.J. Davies (teacher). Middle row: Graham Rogers; Charles Suff; Brian Griffiths; Elfryn Bowen; David Byron Davies; Peter Walke; Eifion Powell (Ferovious); Peter Lewin; Brian Harries; Valerie Williams; Billy Owen. Front row: Trevor Jones; Terry Smith; Mair Rees; John Michael (Androcles); Malcolm Lloyd (Lion); Iris Williams (Louvinia); Ann Suff; Rita Morgan; Alice Jones; Alun Clement.

Alltwen Primary School, Form III, 1929. Back row, left to right: Rhys Samuel; Raymond Davies; Tom Thomas; -?-; Ernie Cook; Tom Price; -?-; Maldwyn Davies; Phil Rees; -?-; John Idwal Roberts; Emlyn Griffiths. Third row: Mr Salmon Mason Thomas (teacher); Molly Rees; Gertie Davies; Miriam Davies; Mair Dilys Davies; Marion James; Martha Rees; Iris Mumford; -?-; Dotia Evans; Nancy Morris; Phylis Jones. Second row: Hilda Hill; Phyllis Jenkins; Doreen Davies; Katie Evans; Gwyneth Rees; Hilda Joseph; Kate Rees; Dilys Jones; Norah Crowley; Evelyn Davies; Nancy Williams; -?-; Ella John; Ceinwen Davies; Jack Williams. Front row: Vincent Rees; Lewis John Lewis; -?-; -?-; Peggy Parry; Elsie Griffiths; Maimie Humphreys; Glenys Howells; Edie Mary Powell; Meg Davies; Mansel Evans; Keith Owen.

Kitchen staff, Alltwen Primary School, c. 1950. From left to right: Mrs Evans; Mrs Laura Williams; Mrs Katie Yates; and Mrs Tilly Humphries.

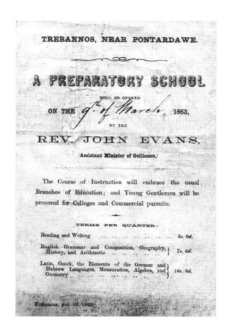

A leaflet issued by the proprietor of a new preparatory school in Trebanos in 1863 by the Revd John Evans, Assistant Minister of Gellionen Unitarian Chapel. The basic reading and writing course cost 5s; the English grammar and composition, geography, history and arithmetic course was 7s 6d; whilst Latin, Greek, German and Hebrew, together with Algebra and Geometry totalled 10s 6d.

Trebanos Infants and Junior School 1937. The infants school was opened in 1910 and the junior department in 1915. Erected on Graig Trebanos, it occupies a prominent site in Trebanos overlooking the busy Swansea Road. Thousands of children have been educated here over the last 100 years.

Children receiving their cycling proficiency certificates at the Pontardawe Rural District Council's office in Holly Street, 31 August 1962. The certificates were awarded by the Chairman of the Council's Road Safety Committee, Mr Evans, in recognition of cycling ability and 'roadmanship' during tests held at the Secondary Modern School in Pontardawe. Graham Joseph, who attended Pontardawe Infants School, is on the far left in the front row, aged five. Baryan Joseph, who is between the two adults in the back row, attended the Secondary Modern. The pupils practised in the schoolyard of the 'Sec Mod' on Saturday mornings and were coached by a local policeman.

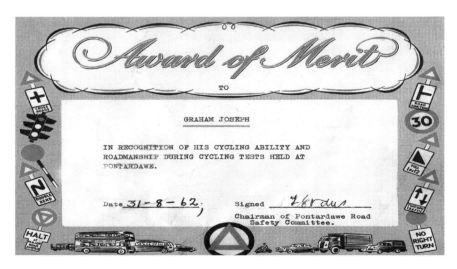

The cycling proficiency certificate.

11

PERSONALITIES

'Asbestos Bill' (William Evans of Fuller Street), demonstrating his athleticism by jumping over an oil drum in the sheetworks in 1954 when aged seventy-four. As head of the annealing department of the sheetworks, he retired in August 1956 after completing sixty-four years in the trade – thirty-two years in the sheetworks and an earlier thirty-two years in the tinplate works. His father and grandfather worked in tinplate before him and when he started at the age of twelve he earned 8*d* a day. Bill enjoyed splendid health throughout his life. When asked what he attributed this to, he said, 'Singing, man. It does you the world of good.'

The gravestone of Richard Thomas of
Gelligron (1631–1715) is one of the
oldest in the district. It lies in the porch of
Llangiwg church and relates to one of the
most powerful landowners in pre-industrial
Pontardawe. Long before the Gilbertsons,
Gelligron was the ancestral home of
the Thomas family. The monumental
inscription records Richard being
married to Katherine, daughter of Lewis
Thomas of Maes Eglwys, a farm in the
parish of Llangyfelach. In Richard's
will of 1712, however, his wife was
named as Joan. Richard was interred in
Llangiwg churchyard on 1 August 1715.
(Royal Commission on the Ancient and
Historical Monuments of Wales)

John Morgan of Gelligron
(1802/3–67) was co-owner of
the Primrose Colliery Co. along
with his brother-in-law Griffith
Lewis of Alltacham (1814–87).
This included the Wauncoed,
Cwmnantllwyd and New
Primrose collieries. They also
owned the Ynysmeudwy Pottery
between 1861 and 1871. John
Morgan lived at Gelligron House
and was buried in Llangiwg
churchyard. His cenotaph is
the tallest, with the inscription
*Erected By The Workers At
the Primrose Collieries And A
Few Friends*.

John Gwyn Jeffreys owned the Gelligron estate in the latter part of the nineteenth century. Although Gelligron was one of his official residences, he was seemingly not there a great deal due to his many biological and maritime activities and expeditions. He was an expert conchologist and marine scientist, as well as a pioneer of deep sea dredging. Much of the former estate lands have now been built over with housing, comprising Waun Penlan, Waun Sterw, Gellideg, Londeg, Cefnllan and Gelliderw.

The Revd Phillip Griffiths was born on 23 January 1793 near Melincourt, Neath, and was a member of Melincourt Independent Chapel. In 1821 he was being taught by the Revd Dr Thomas Phillips and in 1822 accepted a call to the ministry at Pant-teg Independent Chapel in Ystalyfera as well as Alltwen and Carmel, Gwaun-Cae-Gurwen. He also ministered at Bethesda, Ynysmeudwy. He lived in Alltwen (Cwm Llygod, also known as Tyn-y-cae Farm) and served Pant-teg and Alltwen until 1865, and Ynysmeudwy until 1876. Until his death in 1882 he ministered solely at Alltwen. He was one of the most respected ministers in South Wales and wrote many articles for the *Diwygiwr* magazine. He died in 1882 and was the father of Griffith Griffiths of Bryncelyn, Pontardawe, having buried nine other children.

Margaret James, born in Ynysmeudwy in 1903, was member of Tabernacle Chapel, Pontardawe, and became very involved in its cultural activities. She was a gifted elocutionist and teacher who won many recitation competitions in local and national eisteddfodau. Her greatest success was in 1922, when she won the recitation prize at the Ammanford National Eisteddfod using the pseudonym *Merch y Meudwy* (daughter of the hermit). She died in 1985.

Maimie Williams (*née* Humphries) was born in 1918 and educated at Alltwen Primary School and Ystalyfera Intermediate School, before becoming a teacher graduating from Barry Training College. She moved to London where she taught at Croxley School, near Watford, before returning to Clydach Junior School at the end of her teaching career. Maimie was a member of Tabernacle Chapel, Pontardawe, where she was actively involved in local drama productions and became a locally renowned actress, becoming a member of the Swansea Welsh Drama Society. Maimie is best known as a 'Double National Winner' by winning the recitation prizes at Aberpennar (Mountain Ash) National Eisteddfod in 1946 and at the Caerphilly National Eisteddfod in 1950. She died in 1984.

David John Jones ('Dai Tenor') worked as a doubler in the Pontardawe tinplate works and was found to have a brilliant tenor voice by W.D. Clee (the renowned Ystalyfera choirmaster and organist). After winning the Champion Solo competition at the Ammanford National Eisteddfod, he was invited to join the Carl Rosa Opera Company. In the mid-1930s, Dai made an impressive tour of South Africa but his career was cruelly curtailed by the Second World War. He restarted his career after 1945 performing nationwide in concerts, operas and oratorios as well as broadcasting on programmes such as *Welsh Rarebit*, *Golden Chords* and *Grand Hotel*. During the 1950s, Dai sang the title role in Gounod's *Faust* in Cork. The photograph shows Dai as Don Carlos in the Dublin production of that opera in 1950. The Italian soprano, Serafina de Leo, sings with him. Dai spent the autumn of his life as a park-keeper in Pontardawe.

Mary Jones undertook major roles in every Gilbert and Sullivan production by the Pontardawe Operatic Society during the late 1940s and '50s. The photo shows Mary as Phoebe, sitting by her spinning wheel at the opening of *Yeomen of the Guard*. Her performance was described as that of a talented actress with a beautiful mezzo voice. She also took part in many plays performed by the Swansea Drama Society and appeared in radio and TV plays during the 1950s and '60s. Mary devoted a great deal of her life to Tabernacle Chapel contributing to the dramas, concerts and eisteddfodau. Her contribution to the children's Sunday School was immense. Mary was married to Dai ('Tenor') Jones and together they had one son, Trevor, who was himself acclaimed as the best actor in the under-19s drama competition at the National Eisteddfod in Caerphilly during the 1950s. Mary died on 9 June 1994.

Isaac Rees with his wife Mary (*née* Evans) *c*. 1900. Isaac worked at the Bryn tinplate works, Ynysmeudwy, as an engineer on the horizontal steam engine, a machine that drove all the hot mills and the cold rolls in the works. Both Isaac and Mary were born in 1846 and were from Ravenhill, Swansea. They married in 1875. After retirement, Isaac did periodic work at Ynysmeudwy Uchaf Farm for a further four years, repairing milk churns and farm machinery. He died in 1935.

Charlie 'Pots' *c*. 1950. Charlie worked at the chemical works' ruins in Pontardawe. He earned his nickname because he repaired pots, pans and other kitchen utensils. Food cooked in cast iron or aluminium pans developed holes burnt in their bases because of too high a heat. Charlie repaired them by cutting out pieces of tinplate and riveting a metal patch over the holes. He is shown cutting up strips of tinplate with a metal snips. A portable anvil is in front of him, on which he riveted the metal patches onto the pots.

T. George Steadman (*b*. 1877/8) was the son of Thomas Steadman (*b*. 1849/50) who was landlord of the Ivy Bush Hotel in Pontardawe in 1881. T.G. Steadman took over as landlord of the Ivy Bush until 1907/8. According to the Pontardawe historian J.E. Morgan, Thomas Steadman was born in Marden, Herefordshire, which was the place of origin for this major branch of the family in Pontardawe. Another branch hailed from Bethnal Green, London.

Harry Tipping was the people's warden at Llangiwg parish church. A member of the old and respected Tipping family of Rhyd-y-fro, Harry looked after the church and churchyard, keeping everything in perfect order. He also ensured that the paths leading to the church were kept clear and in good condition. The wood to the north-west of the church is still known locally as Tipping's Wood. Harry died in 1976 aged seventy and was buried with his wife, Hilda, in Llangiwg churchyard.

Samuel Yateman Howard c. 1978. Sam was one of the founding members of the Swansea Valley History Society and is shown here at the inaugural exhibition of the Society at the Cross Community Centre in Pontardawe, with some of the working steam models he had made in the kitchen of his home in Godre'r Graig. Sam was a gifted and talented man, quiet and unassuming.

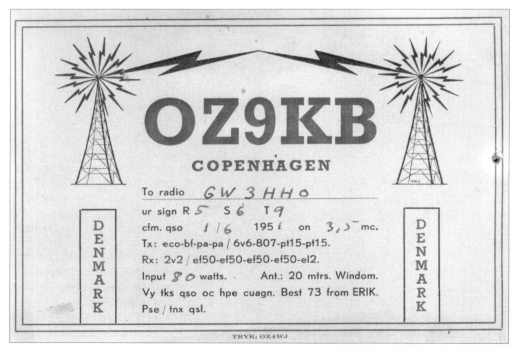

Sam was also a radio ham (amateur radio operator), who had a radio set up in a small shed in his garden at The Croft in Godre'r Graig. His equipment was a radio set previously installed in a wartime aircraft. His call sign was GW3HHO. Sam contacted countries all over Europe by Morse code, including Denmark, Germany, Switzerland, Holland, and Norway.

12

SPORT AND RECREATION

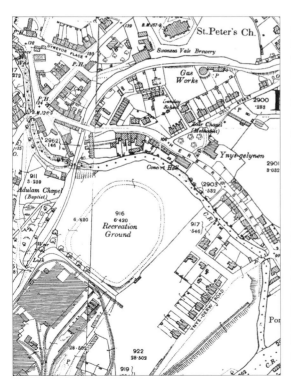

An extract from the Ordnance Survey map of 1901 showing the earliest sports and recreation ground of W. Gilbertson and Co. As well as an athletics track, other sports were also played at the recreation ground, including rugby union and cricket. The recreation ground was also a venue for tennis, and some still refer to the 'Tennis Field' which lay in close vicinity to the top of Francis Street. The recreation ground was overlain by the steelworks from about 1910, the earliest part of which is shown immediately to its left. The steelworks was next to the original tinplate works. The map also shows the incipient development of Ynisderw Road and Francis Street. The steelworks came to cover much of the former recreation ground, the site today being taken up by Lidl supermarket (opened *c.* 2001) and the Pontardawe Retail Park (opened 2008). (Ordnance Survey)

Pontardawe Cricket Club versus a representative Glamorgan County Cricket Club XI, 18 July 1958. The match had been arranged as part of the town's contribution to the Festival of Wales celebrations that week, held to commemorate the British Empire and Commonwealth Games which opened in Cardiff on the same day that year. Among those playing for Glamorgan are Brian Edrich (captain), Jeff Jones, Euros Lewis and Don Ward. Edward Bevan captained Pontardawe who also included D.T. Davies, John James, Tudor Jeremiah and C. Knowles.

Looking scrupulously at the wicket on the occasion of the Festival of Wales match, from left to right, are: Cllr Gilbert Davies; Don Ward; Brian Edrich; and Tom Howell (groundsman). Edrich was assistant coach of Glamorgan at the time having played for the county's First Eleven between 1954 and 1956. He was the brother of Bill, Eric and Geoff Edrich and cousin of John Edrich. Ward played for Glamorgan between 1954 and 1962. He later played club cricket, including a spell at Pontardawe.

Scorecard of a cricket match between Pontardawe and Cowbridge on 5 August 1931 as reported by the *Western Mail & South Wales News*. It describes the then England Test captain, Douglas Jardine, batting last for Cowbridge and being caught and bowled by Lloyd Evans for 26 runs. Jardine scored all the runs in the last wicket partnership with Evans, and was presented with the match ball for his achievement. Jardine's appearance created much interest; this was a year or so before he led England on its notorious 'Bodyline' tour to Australia. The match, which Pontardawe won handsomely, was twelve-a-side, which accounts for eleven wickets being taken by two Pontardawe bowlers. Prominent in the Pontardawe side was Charles Gilbertson, his two sons (Arthur and John), his nephew (William), his brother-in-law (Howel Gwyn Moore-Gwyn), Arthur Suff and Capel Bubb.

CLUB GAMES.

D. R. JARDINE AT PONTARDAWE.

TEST CAPTAIN PLAYS FOR COWBRIDGE.

Mr. D. R. Jardine, the English Test captain, put in an appearance at the Pontardawe v. Cowbridge match, played at Pontardawe on Wednesday, and was prevailed upon to play for the visitors. Mr. Jardine gave a forceful display before he was caught and bowled by Lloyd Evans.

Evans was presented with the ball with which he bowled and caught Jardine. Evans was also in great form with the bat and scored 50 not out. He took four wickets for 13 runs, whilst W. M. Jones took six wickets for 17. Scores:—

PONTARDAWE.

W. M. Jones, lbw, b Sir G. Byass, Bart.	24
R. Morris, lbw, b A. A. Best	44
A. G. Suff, c Spencer, b L. E. Williams	4
Major Moore Gwyn, st Bird, b Pritchard	42
A. G. Gilbertson, c Best, b Pritchard	7
W. F. Gilbertson, c Best, b Pritchard	5
J. Aldridge, c Sir G. Byass, Bart., b S. Evans	20
Ll. Evans, not out	50
J. Gilbertson, b L. E. Williams	3
A. C. Bubb, not out	7
Extras	2

Total (for eight. dec.) 209

COWBRIDGE.

L. E. Williams, c and b Evans	11
B. S. Bird, b W. M. Jones	0
C. E. Dixon, c C. Gilbertson, b Jones	4
W. I. Williams, c Aldridge, b Evans	10
Sir G. Byass, Bart, b Jones	2
F. E. Dunn, c Evans, b Jones	0
R. A. Byass, b Evans	5
A. A. Best, c Morris, b Jones	1
A. Spencer, b Jones	0
F. Williams, b Jones	0
D. C. Pritchard, not out	6
D. R. Jardine, c and b Evans	26
Extras	2

Total 67

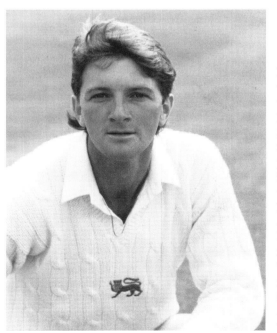

Born in 1960 in Trebanos, Greg Thomas was a fast bowler of genuine pace who played cricket for Glamorgan and Northamptonshire, as well as representing England at Test level. He made his debut for his home county in 1979. He won a place on England's tour to the West Indies in 1985/86, and in his first Test, almost took a wicket with his first two deliveries to Desmond Haynes. In all, he played five Tests and three one-day internationals for England, as well as 192 first class matches for Glamorgan and Northamptonshire. Thomas participated in 183 List A matches for both counties, and also played cricket for Border and Eastern Province in South Africa. He was forced to retire at the end of the 1991 season due to injury.

Phil Hopkins first played rugby
union at school level for Pontardawe
Collegiate School (Tanyrallt House), and
subsequently for the University College
of North Wales, Bangor. At club level,
Phil played rugby for Pontardawe RFC
before switching to Swansea. In 1908,
he was capped against Australia and
scored a try in a narrow victory. A wing,
he next played for Wales in 1909 against
England and Ireland, scoring a try in
both games, and helping Wales to win
the Triple Crown. He played in just one
more match for Wales, against England
in 1910. Phil also excelled at hockey,
golf and tennis. He died in September
1966 and is buried in All Saints
churchyard.

Gwilym Michael was born in Pontardawe
in 1892. He started playing for
Pontardawe RFC in 1919, and by 1921
was in the Swansea team. A flank
forward, he was first capped for Wales
against England in 1923, and went on to
play against Scotland and France in that
year. He was also chosen to be a part of a
combined England and Wales side, playing
against Scotland and Ireland to mark 100
years since Webb Ellis's introduction of
rugby as it is known today. The match
was played at the famous Rugby Public
School. Gwilym died in May 1941.

Edgar Morgan was born in Pontardawe on 15 April 1882, and educated at the Pontardawe Collegiate School and University College of North Wales, Bangor. He played for Alltwen RFC and Pontardawe RFC. He then joined Swansea RFC, and was part of the team that defeated Australia (1908) and South Africa (1912). Edgar was first capped by the Anglo-Welsh British Lions team that toured Australia and New Zealand in 1908. He gained two caps as a hooker on the tour, in which he made a total of fourteen appearances on the New Zealand leg. He had to wait another six years for his first Welsh cap which was against England in January 1914 – he subsequently played against Scotland and Ireland. The Irish match became infamous for its battle of the forwards with the Welsh pack afterwards being dubbed 'The Terrible Eight'. Edgar's last international match was against France in 1914 in Swansea. He joined the Army at the outbreak of the First World War, and was awarded the Military Cross. He died in 1962.

Keri Jones, a native of Alltwen, won his first senior Welsh rugby union cap when he played against New Zealand at Cardiff Arms Park on 11 November 1967, on the left wing. Educated at Ystalyfera Grammar School and Cardiff College of Education, he had played in this position since his schooldays, gaining caps for the Welsh Secondary Schools in the 1962/63 season. In 1966 he represented Wales at the Commonwealth Games in Jamaica in the relay and 100 and 220 yard sprints. Keri played for Neath RFC and Cardiff College of Education before joining Cardiff. He won a total of five Welsh caps between 1967 and 1968.

Members of Pontardawe RFC at their annual dinner held at the Mackworth Hotel, Swansea, *c.* 1953. Included in the photograph are: Alf Bishop; Tom Bowen; John Carney snr; Alex Chapman; Islwyn Davies; Milton Davies; Des Flook; Meurig George; Ron Griffiths; Roy Harris; Charlie Heaver; Jeff Hopkins; Tom Howell; Richard Howells; Vic James; Jackie Jones; Joe Jones; Les Jones; Bill Lewis; Ken Lewis; Tom Lewis; John Price; Len Pugh; Des Rapsey; Ken Rees; Emlyn Thomas; and Evan Williams.

Pontardawe RFC, 1892/93. Taken eleven years after the official formation of the club in 1881, the side was largely composed of workers from Gilbertson's works in Pontardawe. For many years the club used various public houses in Pontardawe as its headquarters before moving, in 1979, to a purpose-built clubhouse in Ynisderw Road. The player with the cap on the right of the front row may be either Jack Cumberland or Syd Edwards, both of whom represented the Glamorgan County Rugby Club.

Trebanos RFC, 1950s, setting out on a tour to Bristol. Those present include: back row, left to right: William Thomas; -?- (bus driver); Gwyn Williams; Doug Davies; Jackie Jones; Dick Lewis; Lando Joseph; Thomas Henry Jones; Lyn Davies; Howard James; Bryn Williams; Dillwyn Hughes; Will Tom James; Danny Williams; Cliff Jones; Arthur Jones; Gwyn Morgan; Islwyn Phillips; Herbert Thomas; Dai 'Kid' Jones; Bryn 'Socks' Williams; Len Thomas; Emrys Lewis. Front row: Danny Walters; Jack Lewis; Glan Lewis; Gomer Davies; Glyn Jenkins; Tom Jones; John Lewis; Ken Davies; Ceri Davies; Byron Hopkin.

Alltwen RFC, 1960/61. Back row, left to right: -?-; Keri Jones; Geogh Maddox; Colin Wilde; Brian Nelson; Glan Williams; Viv Phillips; -?-. Front row: Stephen Getvoldsen; Keith Day; Reggie Jones; Keith Parfitt (captain); -?-; Islwyn Jenkins; David Williams. Keri Jones is seen here in his grammar school days, before he went to Cardiff College of Education.

Pontardawe AFC, 1961/62. Standing, left to right: Dave Knight; Roy Hopkins; Gwyn Davies; Clasfryn Bowen; Huw Rees; Raymond Cook; Dai Trollope; Dickie Davies (Chairman). Sitting: Tudor Jeremiah; Eric Lewis; Dick Evans; Dewi Lewis; Mike Hudson.

Alltwen United AFC, c. 1930s. Included in the photograph are: Jim Rengozzi; Leslie Gibbon; Gwyn Evans; Leslie Lewis; Archie Head; Garfield Evans; Austin Evans; Patrick Hennessy. The photograph was taken outside the former Cross Hands public house that was located at the bottom of Alltwen Hill and was demolished in 1974.

Pontardawe Cycling, Sports and Athletics Club, 1898, seen here at the original recreation ground. The five-seat bicycle was known as a 'quinary', derived from 'quint-racing' (the sport of racing five-seaters), and was a popular form of cycle racing at the time. The playing field and the running track within the recreation ground were used by a variety of sportsmen in the community.

Roller skating at the Rink, Works Lane, Pontardawe. The Rink was run by Lewis Bros, local mineral water manufacturers who were based in Grove Road. The Rink opened as a roller skating hall and later became a dance hall (the *Palais de Danse*). The land on which the Rink stands was leased to Lewis Bros. The building still stands and is now a nightclub – the *Paradise Club*, formerly *Mamma Mia's*.

Above: Evelyn Davies, demonstrating her golfing prowess to friends. Evelyn worked as a typist in the steel works in Pontardawe, and this photograph was taken on waste ground close to the works' canteen. Also included in the photograph are Rene John (left), Gwen Pugh (holding the other golf club), Jean Williams and Betty Hopkins. Evelyn was captain of the Ladies Section of Pontardawe Golf Club in 1956, about the time this photograph was taken. In the background is Chemical Works Lane with the goods shed of Pontardawe railway station above.

Left: Marilyn Pugh (*née* Morgan), from Lower Brynamman but living in Gellinudd today, was an accomplished hockey player winning ninety senior caps for Wales, the first of which was against Ireland in 1973. She also represented Great Britain twenty-five times, becoming vice captain and playing in many World Championship games. Her greatest regret was not being able to participate in the 1980 Moscow Olympics, as the national (GB) hockey team had boycotted the games in protest against the Soviet Union's invasion of Afghanistan the previous year.

13

SOCIAL AND CULTURAL ACTIVITIES

Opening ceremony of Pontardawe Workmen's Club and Institute, 31 May 1930. The contractor, Roger H. Thomas (centre left), hands the keys to Dr Constant Gustav Logan Dahne (centre) who performed the opening. Dr Dahne (1866–1934), who was of Danish-German descent, was well-known in the Pontardawe district where he practised for over thirty-three years at the time of his death, and where he was 'greatly respected'. He and his family lived in Gwynfa, Maes Iago and earlier at *The Laurels*, the property which became the Royal British Legion Club (now The Other Place), on Ynisderw Road.

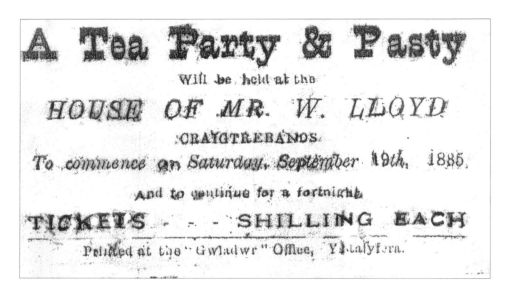

A bidding card from Trebanos, 1885. The card's dimensions are 3in by 1¾in and printed by the Gwladwr Press of Ystalyfera for Mr and Mrs Williams. The purpose of such cards was to raise money for a newly-wed couple to set up home together. A cup of tea and a pasty for 1s, on sale for two weeks, allowed the would-be couple's friends and family to visit the house and contribute to the money fund. One shilling then equates with £10 today.

Bob Williams the Marriage Man. Bob is the last Marriage Man in Wales. He performed his first ceremony in 1980, when he resurrected the ancient marriage ceremony of jumping the broom. In the past, before official marriage ceremonies came to the more remote parts of Wales, a Marriage Man would announce a couple wed if they jumped over a broom. The Marriage Man raised the broom, and then laid it on the floor. The couple jumped the broom three times; forward and back, then forward again whilst holding hands, implying marriage was not to be taken lightly. The final leap forward was to symbolise jumping into their new life together.

The last trustees of the Pontardawe Public Hall and Institute, *c.* 1994. From left to right: Eurig Roberts; John Moses; David Lewis; William Davies; Dewi Davies; and Richard Strange. The Public Hall and Institute was officially opened by Baroness Cederström (Dame Adelina Patti) on 6 May 1909, and accommodated 1,700 users. The building closed in 1994, with the lease of the building being taken over by Lliw Valley Borough Council. It was reopened as the Pontardawe Arts Centre in October 1996.

Versey Evans, owner of the Rose-Lynne Nursery at Brondeg Lane, Alltwen, proudly shows his floral display at the horticultural and arts and crafts show held at Pontardawe sheetworks in 1958. Versey, a sheetworks employee, was an expert gardener and horticulturalist who won many awards. Among the display are dahlias, chrysanthemums, carnations, asparagus fern and goldenrod.

The Pontardawe International Music Festival parade 1984, held in the High Street, showing the Pontardawe-based folk dance team Cam Carlam, formed in 1983. In the photograph from left to right are: Beata Gegenwart; Barry Rendel; Celia and John Lauday; Marion Davies; Clive Reed (one of the co-authors of this volume) and Huw Jones the melodeon player, with his daughter Claire. Sadly, the Festival, which was run entirely by volunteers, ended in 2010.

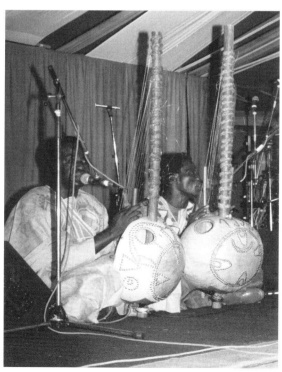

Kausa Kuyateh (left) and Dembo Konte (right) at the Pontardawe International Music Festival 1983. The Festival brought a huge variety of music to Pontardawe from nations all over the world. The artists who appeared at Pontardawe were highly regarded, and among the most celebrated artists in their own countries. Foremost among these, from Gambia in West Africa, came Dembo Konte and Kausa Kuyateh who played the Kora, a twenty-one-string harp-lute. Zi Lan Liao and Guo Yue from China and Marta Sebestyén from Hungary also featured.

Ruth Exell Stevenson. Ruth plays the Celtic harp and is a singer of traditional folk music. She has sung with a number of folk groups, including Strumpet and Will Griffy's Music, and performed in France, Spain, and all over the UK. She is one of the founding members of the Pontardawe Folk Festival, to which she gave many years of unpaid work as a director, artistic manager and an artist in her own right. The photograph shows Ruth in Brittany in 1992, at the twinning of the Pontardawe and Monterfil folk festivals.

Lynne Gent, folk singer of Pontardawe. Manchester-born Lynne is a fine singer of traditional and contemporary songs, performing in folk clubs and other venues in Wales, England, France and Spain for over forty years. She performs mostly as a solo artist, but has also sung with the local folk groups Swansea Jack and Strumpet, and features on a number of records, tapes and CDs. Founder chairperson of the Pontardawe Folk Festival at which she sang as an artist, she later designed and created the fantastic backdrops to the main stage. The photograph shows Lynne at a Breton festival in June 1992.

The Rhos Welsh Dramatic Society, pictured here in 1910, was typical of the societies that were active in the various villages of the district, putting on performances in chapel and church halls as well as the Public Hall. Those shown include back row, left to right: F. Powell (Treasurer); D.R. Lewis; J.D. Williams; L. John; L. Williams; H. Jenkins; Thomas Gibbs; S. Jenkins; D.R. Williams; L.J. Williams (Secretary). Middle row: -?-; T.W. Davies; E. Jones; L. Francis; B. John; A.J. Williams; A. Williams; J.E. Thomas; D.M. Davies. Front row: D.J. Williams (Chairman); G. Jenkins; C. Williams; D.L. Jenkins (Conductor); Sarah Davies; Maggie Williams; J.S. Jenkins; H. Edmunds.

The Tarenni Colliery Brass Band are photographed here outside Llangiwg School (the 'Girls School') in Brecon Road, (date unknown), showing the victory shields won in competition. Included in the photograph are back row, left to right: D. Landry; E.T. Lewis; D. Jones; W. Jones; R. Jones; C. Francis; D.W.R. Walker; E. Davies. Second row: W.J. Williams; A. Williams; J.L. Rees; D.R. Williams; C. Williams; D.R. Todd; J.T. Williams; W.H. Todd; E. Thomas. Front row: J. Roderick; T. Clee; B.I. Davies; T. Dixon (President and Managing Director, Tarenni Colliery); T.E. Jones (conductor); L.W. Williams; B. Davies; W.A. Williams; R .Morgans. Sitting at the front is E.G. Lewis.

14

IMAGES OF WARTIME

Trooper Frank Hopkins (No. 1983) of the 9th Lancers lived in Maes Iago, Pontardawe, and served in Afghanistan between 1878 and 1880, during the Second Anglo-Afghan War. This conflict had its origins in the perennial fear that Russia would invade India. Trooper Hopkins was probably awarded the Kabul to Kandahar Star and an Afghan Campaign Medal with Kandahar Clasp for his service in Afghanistan.

Lance Corporal William John Thomas, was the son of George and Sarah Thomas of Compass Row, Pontardawe, and was decorated in the First World War with the Military Medal. He was a member of the 16th Royal Welsh Fusiliers (no. 54058) and lost his life on 22 April 1918, aged twenty-one. He is buried at Bouzincourt Ridge Cemetery, Albert, France. There is a plaque with his name, along with other chapel members, in Soar Chapel, Pontardawe.

Bryniog (Bryn) Thomas (no. 3910474) initially enlisted in the South Wales Borderers on 15 November 1939, and later transferred to the Durham Light Infantry, serving in Africa, Italy and north-west Europe. He landed in Normandy on D-Day, with the Durham Light Infantry. On 12 June 1944 Bryn was awarded the Military Medal. He later had a milk round covering Pontardawe, Ynysmeudwy, Cilmaengwyn and Godre'r Graig and was known affectionately as 'Bryn the Milk'.

William John Davies ('Willy Lighthouse') was a native of Pontardawe, and was in Montevideo harbour aboard the *SS Lynton Grange* when the German pocket battleship, the *Graff Spee*, was scuttled outside the harbour in 1939. The photograph below shows William (left) on board the *SS Lynton Grange* with another member of the crew in Montevideo harbour, just prior to the sinking of the *Graff Spee*. Although a merchant ship, note the gun on the deck that was used primarily for protection against U-boats. The *Lynton Grange* was torpedoed by U-406 and the ship was abandoned, being sunk by the U-628. The Master, forty-one crew and ten gunners were rescued by HMS *Milne* and landed at Ponta Delgada in the Azores.

Harold Penderel was originally known as E.A.H. Jones and lived at Garth Farm, Rhyd-y-fro. The family changed their name to Penderel in the early 1930s at the request of their mother. Harold was a Second Lieutenant in the Heavy Machine Gun Corps, later to become the Tank Corps. He was mentioned in Despatches on 16 March 1919 by Field Marshall Sir Douglas Haig for gallant and distinguished service in the field, the commendation being signed by Winston Churchill, Secretary of State for War. Harold fought in the Battle of Cambrai in 1917, the first battle which used tanks to spearhead an attack on the enemy without the traditional prolonged bombardment.

The Home Guard, Trebanos detachment. The Home Guard (initially called the Local Defence Volunteers) was operational from 1940 until 1944. As an organisation it comprised 1.5 million local volunteers otherwise ineligible for military service (usually owing to age), hence the nickname 'Dad's Army'. It acted as a secondary defence force, in case of invasion by the German forces and their allies.

John Howard Williams of Alltwen. John, on the right, was born in 1925, and was called up for war service in 1941. He trained in Ireland for mountain warfare and was sent to India on active service. He served with the Devonshire Regiment of the 14th Army in India and Burma between 1942 and 1946, seeing action at Imphal, one of the bitterest battles of the war in the east, and at Mandalay. At the war's end, the Japanese soldiers who had committed atrocities were tried at the Singapore War Crimes Trials, in which John participated. John was a Justice of the Peace from 1966 to 1996. He died in 2008.

Arthur Graham Owens was born on 14 April 1899 in Graig Road, Gellinudd. During the Second World War, he became a double agent (codenamed 'Snow'), working for both the German and British Intelligence Services. He became the first of the great double-cross agents who were to play a major part in Britain's victory over the Germans. His extraordinary story is told in a recent book entitled *Snow*, written by Nigel West and Madoc Roberts. Arthur's daughter, Patricia Owens, became a Hollywood film actress and is best remembered for her role in *The Fly* (1958). Arthur died on 24 December 1957 and is buried in Wexford, Ireland.

Emlyn Williams of Pontardawe. Emlyn was born in 1923, and worked at Glantawe tinplate works and the Garth colliery, near Glais. He enlisted in the Royal Air Force in 1942 and completed one year's training at an air gunnery school near Inverness before moving to an operational training unit in 1944, flying Wellington medium bombers. He was given the rank of Sergeant Air Gunner, manning the mid-upper gun turret in a Lancaster Bomber. Emlyn served with 50 Squadron RAF during the Second World War and flew with the same crew throughout, suffering no casualties.

(including results of bombing, gunnery, exercises, etc.)

No.
28. OPERATIONS. LADBERGEN.   15,250.ft
29. OPERATIONS. HARBURG.   13,750ft
30. OPERATIONS. ESSEN.   16,750ft
31. OPERATIONS. DORTMUND.   15,250ft
    AIR TEST.
32 OPERATIONS. WORZBURG.   9.250.ft
    FIGHTER AFFIL

Emlyn's logbook showed that his first air raid was in September 1944. In all, he flew in thirty-five air raids over Europe. The longest time in the air was of eleven hours, after his aircraft was damaged by enemy anti-aircraft fire. His aircraft bombed many industrial sites including U-boat pens, dams in the Ruhr Valley and raids to Essen, Dortmund and Munich, where he spent his twenty-first birthday bombarding the city. He remembered numerous collisions in the air, but considered himself to have been a lucky person, only having one crash. The last air raid Emlyn flew was on 4 April 1945, to Nordhausen.